For Christ and Covenant

Classics of Reformed Spirituality
Michael A.G. Haykin, series editor

To honour God:
The spirituality of Oliver Cromwell
Michael A.G. Haykin, Ed.

The revived Puritan:
The spirituality of George Whitefield
Michael A.G. Haykin, Ed.

The armies of the Lamb:
The spirituality of Andrew Fuller
Michael A.G. Haykin, Ed.

For Christ and Covenant:
The spirituality of Archibald Johnston of Wariston
Ruth E. Alcalay, Ed.

Classics of Reformed Spirituality

For Christ and Covenant

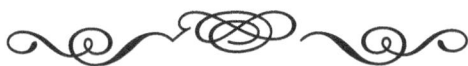

*The spirituality of
Archibald Johnston
of Wariston*

Edited and introduced by
Ruth E. Alcalay

joshua
press

jOshUa
p r e s s

www.joshuapress.com

Published by
Joshua Press Inc., Kitchener, Ontario, Canada
Distributed by
Sola Scriptura Ministries International
www.sola-scriptura.ca

First published in 2011.

The publication of this book was made possible by the generous support of:
The Ross-Shire Foundation
& Geneva College (Beaver Falls, PA)

© 2011 Cover and book design by Janice Van Eck
Cover illustration by Deborah Livingston-Lowe
Portrait of Lord Wariston based on the portrait by George Jamesone

———

Library and Archives Canada Cataloguing in Publication

Warriston, Archibald Johnston, Lord, 1611–1663
For Christ and Covenant : the spirituality of Archibald Johnston
of Wariston / edited and introduced by Ruth E. Alcalay.

(Classics of Reformed spirituality)
Includes bibliographical references

ISBN 978-1-894400-36-7

1. Warriston, Archibald Johnston, Lord, 1611-1663—Religion.
2. Covenanters—Scotland—Biography. 3. Statesmen—Scotland—Biography.
I. Mayers, Ruth E. (Ruth Elisabeth), 1972– II. Title.
III. Series: Classics of Reformed spirituality

BX9225.W35A25 2011   285'.2092   C2011-901045-3

For Eugene, with love always

Contents

Editorial note

Archibald Johnston wrote his diary in a broad Lowland Scots dialect, which is not readily accessible to the modern reader. Sentences tend to be long, rambling and repetitive, with little punctuation. I have therefore anglicized and modernized spellings, translated Scottish words, inserted punctuation and omitted some subordinate clauses for the sake of clarity. Johnston's use of the second person singular (thee/thou) has been retained. Words in square brackets have been added for clarification and references to dates and Scripture passages have been simplified.

For Christ and Covenant

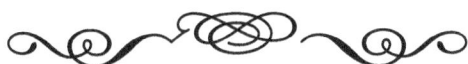

The spirituality of Archibald Johnston of Wariston

1611–1663

Archibald Johnston of Wariston was, undoubtedly, one of mid-seventeenth-century Scotland's most influential religious and political figures. A talented, godly, yet comparatively obscure young lawyer, he joined the resistance to the ecclesiastical innovations of Charles I in 1637, and rapidly emerged as a leader among the reformers who effectively ruled Scotland for most of the next fourteen years. Co-author of the Scottish National Covenant of 1638, Johnston went on to negotiate the Solemn League and Covenant with England's Long Parliament in 1643, serve on the Committee of Both Kingdoms that managed the war effort and participate in the Westminster Assembly. After some years of retirement, consequent upon Covenanter fragmentation and the English conquest of Scotland, Johnston was reconciled to Oliver Cromwell and resumed activity on the British political stage. His career climaxed in 1659, when he became president of the Council of State, administering the united Commonwealth of England, Scotland and

Ireland. Power and prominence did not, however, produce popularity. Though a minority honoured him as a "sincere, fervent seeker of God," by 1660 Johnston found himself the object of widespread "hatred and indignation," which facilitated his subsequent execution at the behest of a resurgent and vindictive monarchy under Charles II.[1]

Controversy has continued to surround Johnston's posthumous reputation. For the persecuted Covenanters and their radical Presbyterian descendants, he remained a heroic martyr in Christ's cause.[2] Conversely, their episcopalian opponents remembered him as a treacherous hypocrite who fully deserved his fate. Among the first to sense the complex reality behind contemporary caricatures was the nineteenth-century historian Thomas Carlyle, who described him as a "canny lynx-eyed Lawyer and austere Presbyterian Zealot; full of fire, of heavy energy and gloom."[3] The recovery of substantial sections of his intimate personal diary has only strengthened the trend towards contradictory representations.[4]

Modern scholars have rightly criticized reductionist partisan portraits of a "sanitized saint," but their own attempts to reach a

---

1   *The last discourse of the Right Honourable the Lord Warestoune, as he delivered it upon the scaffold at the Mercat-Cross of Edinburgh, July 22, 1663, being immediately before his death* (Edinburgh, 1664), 3; J.D. Ogilvie, ed., *The Diary of Sir Archibald Johnston of Wariston, 1655–1660* (Edinburgh: Scottish History Society, 1940), 182.

2   See for example the brief account by John Howie of Lochgoin, who introduced himself as a lover of the "same cause," and recalled the "sweet fellowship" that had existed between his ancestors and those he included in *The Scots Worthies* (1775) [Repr. Edinburgh: The Banner of Truth Trust, 1995]. Howie drew heavily on Robert Wodrow, *The History of the Sufferings of the Church of Scotland from the Restoration to the Revolution* (1721/1722); Wodrow (1679–1734) was himself the son of a Covenanting preacher.

3   Thomas Carlyle, *Oliver Cromwell's Letters and Speeches, with Elucidations* (London: Chapman & Hall, 1845), II:301.

4   Although the diary's existence was known to a few eighteenth-century writers, including James Howie, who described the manuscript as "a valuable treasure both of Christian experience and matters of fact" (*Scots Worthies*, 315), it was not published until the early twentieth century.

more balanced understanding are equally flawed by prejudice. Although he acknowledges Johnston's "ability and energy," David Stevenson, the premier historian of the Covenanting period, sees much merit in the "hostile verdict" on this "archetype of the grim Calvinist," whom he depicts as a "deeply unpleasant man" afflicted with "severe mental disorder."[5] Edmund Cowan, similarly, posits a "huge gulf between Johnston's private and public personae," and even suggests that the diary's emotional content and "convoluted... obtuse" prose indicate that the writer was a "religious maniac"[6]! Greater familiarity with the religious context enables Louise Yeoman to perceive that Johnston was not, by contemporary standards, insane; superficially more sympathetic, she suggests that it is "not so much" the man as his "version of God" that "can come across to us as a monster."[7] Behind such negative judgements lies a profound antipathy to, and incomprehension of, Archibald Johnston's spirituality. Stevenson does not disguise his contempt for the "mental cage" of "orthodox Calvinism" to which the Covenanters adhered, and doubts that "even the most dour presbyterian supporters" could now view Johnston as "an example to be held up to others of true religion."Yeoman highlights Johnston's "obsession" with discerning God's will, and likens him and other Calvinist parents to Buddhist Zen masters, indifferent to their pupils' suffering.[8]

That unbelieving historians should respond so dismissively is scarcely surprising. More remarkable is the fact that, notwithstand-

5 David Stevenson, "Depression and Salvation: Sir Archibald Johnston of Wariston," in his *King or Covenant?: Voices from Civil War* (East Linton: Tuckwell Press, 1996), 151, 172.

6 Edmund Cowan, "The Making of the National Covenant," in John Morrill, ed., *The Scottish National Covenant in its British Context, 1638–1651* (Edinburgh: Edinburgh University Press, 1990), 76.

7 Louise Yeoman, "Archie's invisible worlds discovered: spirituality, madness and Johnston of Wariston's family," *Records of the Scottish Church History Society* (1997), 158.

8 Stevenson, "Depression and Salvation," 172–173; Yeoman, "Archie's invisible worlds discovered," 157, 161–162.

ing the late-twentieth-century renewal of interest in the Puritans and Covenanters, recent Christian historical writers have allotted little or no space to Johnston.[9] This book is intended to rectify the omission, and disprove Stevenson's contention, by demonstrating that, despite his imperfections, much spiritual benefit may be derived from Johnston's richly documented inner life, whose principal features are surveyed below.

"His wonderful calling": background and conversion

Archibald Johnston was born in March 1611 to a prosperous Edinburgh family, closely connected with the city's mercantile and legal elite. Bereaved of his father James just six years later, Archibald, like Timothy,[10] was raised by a godly mother, Elizabeth Craig, and grandmother, Rachel Arnot. A woman of strong faith in Christ, whose last words confidently affirmed "He will light my candle and lighten my darkness," Elizabeth endeavoured in life to draw her children into the kingdom of heaven.[11] These exertions were not lost on Archibald, who saw himself as the "son of many tears and prayers to her" and attributed his youthful deliverance from "strange taunts and humours" to her intercession.[12] Besides regular attendance at public worship, Archibald's mother and grandmother held frequent private prayer meetings with like-minded friends. Both women also made personal covenants committing them-

---

9 A partial exception is William Barker, who includes a brief account of Johnston in his *Puritan Profiles* (Barker, *Puritan Profiles: 54 Contemporaries of the Westminster Assembly* [Tain: Christian Focus, 2000]), but this relies heavily on Stevenson and the *Dictionary of National Biography* rather than contemporary sources.

10 2 Timothy 1:5.

11 G.M. Paul, ed., *The Diary of Sir Archibald Johnston of Wariston, 1632–1639* (Edinburgh: Scottish History Society, 1911), 125.

12 *Diary, 1655–1660*, 173–174; *Diary, 1632–1639*, 364; Yeoman, "Archie's invisible worlds discovered," 181.

selves and their children to God, and supported the Presbyterian opposition to James VI and I's attempt to bring the Scottish Kirk[13] into closer liturgical and governmental conformity to the Church of England.[14]

Archibald thus grew up in an atmosphere of fervent piety and ecclesiastical controversy, which did much to shape his opinions and character. He afterwards praised the Lord for "making [him] to be of the seed of the faithful" and for "dealing with [him] as a child, melting [his] heart like water at a feast in the new kirk, at the reading of David's tears the second time, and at home another time."[15]

Despite his religious training and early spiritual impressions, Archibald Johnston's recollections reveal that he was not actually saved in childhood. An intelligent and imaginative boy, he habitually failed to tell the "truth, without adding, paring or changing something." While he worked hard to acquire the knowledge necessary for a legal career, his motives were mixed. Looking back, he detected early symptoms of a "proud, ambitious humour" in his eagerness to arrogate precedence over his tutor and outperform others, and saw God's correcting hand in the humiliating setbacks occasioned by frequent, sometimes near-fatal, bouts of illness. In adolescence, Archibald was increasingly swayed by ungodly friends; though preserved from "scandalous acts of lust," he afterwards perceived himself as "drowned in all kind of licentiousness," especially the "foolish talking" and "jesting" forbidden in Ephesians 5:4. But a great change came in May 1626, when the fifteen-year-old experienced God's "wonderful calling" at a communion service, during which

---

13 Meaning, "The Church of Scotland."

14 D.H. Fleming, ed., *The Diary of Sir Archibald Johnston of Wariston, 1650–1654* (Edinburgh: Scottish History Society, 1919), 68; Yeoman, "Archie's invisible worlds discovered," 160. On the reaction to James's religious policies, see P.H.R. Mackay, "The reception given to the Five Articles of Perth," *Records of the Scottish Church History Society* (1977), 185–201.

15 *Diary, 1632–1639,* 125.

he shed "many tears" of repentance and rejoiced in applying to himself such Scriptures as Romans 5:8–10, affirming reconciliation for sinners through the death of Christ. For several weeks thereafter he enjoyed an extraordinary sense of the Lord's presence in prayer "continually every evening and morning in [his] mother's gallery.[16]" Though these raptures eventually faded, Johnston's life was permanently transformed. He would always remember this communion as the occasion of his effectual calling: the "means under God that first took me by the heart," the "first experience of God's hearing my prayers and fulfilling his promises." Other proofs of the divine faithfulness followed. Johnston particularly recalled answered prayer for "direction to [his] studies, and a safe return" from France, where he travelled for three months after graduating from Glasgow University in 1630. He also recalled God "delivering [him] from temptations and blessing [him] so extraordinarily" in the marriage arranged by his family in 1632. His teenage bride, Jean Stewart (d.1633), the daughter of a prominent lawyer, was also an earnest believer: when they discussed spiritual things, Archibald was "ravished with her answers, and blessed God for her." Thus, initial doubts concerning the match soon yielded to deep love and close Christian companionship.[17]

Cataloguing God's mercies: a spirituality centred on memory and meditation

In June 1633, Jean's sudden death after less than eight months of marriage precipitated the first severe trial of Archibald Johnston's faith. Self-denying submission to God's sovereign decree and the "comfort" derived from assurance of "her eternal happiness," did not protect the young widower from acute pain on his own account.

---

16 Meaning "room."

17 *Diary, 1655–1660*, 172; *Diary, 1632–1639*, 378, 72, 125, 1–2; *Diary, 1650–1654*, 271; *Diary, 1632–1639*, 104, 11.

As the weeks passed, his depression worsened: "extreme agony," "unutterable extremity," "unspeakable misery," the "brink of desperation" are just a few of the expressions he used to describe his emotional anguish. Desolate and fearing to fall into temptation now that his wife's removal had "loosed the chain to [his] rash affections," he sometimes longed for death. Grief was aggravated by growth in understanding of his own guilt: realizing as never before the secret faults of the last seven months, he suspected that these had provoked God's anger and led to his bereavement. Worst of all was the feeling that his heavenly Father had withdrawn from him, "as a wicked, ungrateful child," and the "hopeless fear" that this apparent desertion might be perpetual, that he was already "foretasting the torments of hell." Though not a conversion experience, as some have supposed, this furnace of affliction forged or refined important aspects of Johnston's spirituality.[18]

Among the most significant developments of this period was the start of Archibald Johnston's written testimony. Originally an undated series of spiritual reminiscences, this manuscript's central theme, announced in the imperative title—*Memento Quamdiu Vivas* ("Remember as long as you live")—is sanctified memory. Compiling and considering the "doleful catalogue" of his sins and the joyous "catalogue of…bygone mercies" had long been a part of Johnston's Christian life. He now prayed for grace "to see and…to remember all the footsteps" of God in "casting [him] down by this cross of [his] fatherly love." Suffering thus impelled Johnston toward, not away from, the Lord: by writing down former experiences of divine favour he hoped to "strengthen [his] faith in the day of new troubles." Again and again he exhorts his soul to remember these blessings, and in so doing, even at moments of deep dejection, derives material for fervent praise, as well as encouragement to persevere. Not all memories, of course, were pleasant: careful self-

---

18 *Diary, 1655–1660*, 15–16, 58, 56–57, 13, 28, 17, 60.

examination prompted much mourning for past sin. But when oppressed with guilt he also recalled and relied on the promises of pardon through Christ's death, gave thanks for the gift of repentance and trusted that "remembrance of this godly sorrow" might "one day comfort…and uphold [him] in the day of temptation." The great turning point in his struggle for assurance came on Saturday, July 27, 1633. That morning, while meditating in the Scheins-yard in Edinburgh, he was overwhelmed with consciousness of Christ's intercession for him and the Holy Spirit's inner witness to the Father's "free love and gracious mercy pardoning all in the blood of his well-beloved Son." Thereafter, despite continued difficulties, Johnston did not seriously doubt his salvation; the consoling memory of this deliverance would prove a source of strength and impetus to prayer amidst many future perplexities. Such active recollection is a duty clearly required of the Lord's people in Scripture, but few believers are known to have engaged in it with the sustained concentration of Archibald Johnston. The exercise of remembering and recording proved so salutary that he continued it for decades, producing a copious, almost daily chronicle filling several volumes. These diaries he committed to God's "preserving and blessing hand" with gratitude for the "good matter" contained therein and petitions for "much more." By the 1650s, indeed, his conscious purpose in writing extended beyond personal edification to promoting "the glory of [God's] name and the good of his people"—commendable ends that are still being achieved.[19]

Best suited to these goals, and so most memorable in Johnston's estimation, were the Lord's "providences" in external affairs and "influences" on the heart. The former emphasis explains the extraordinary detail of the surviving diaries, which narrate comparatively minor domestic incidents alongside events of obvious national importance. Such comprehensiveness sprang from confidence in

---

19 *Diary, 1655-1660*, 1, 56, 58–59, 66; *Diary, 1650–1654*, 240, 195-196.

the biblical doctrine that nothing happens by chance, since God is still actively governing the universe for his people's ultimate good. Johnston's zealous efforts to discern the significance of specific circumstances, and thus obtain direction—in later years he even resorted to the dubious method of casting lots—may well appear misguided, since Scripture also affirms the limits of human knowledge and the mystery of divine sovereignty.[20] Yet his faith that meaning exists in history, and his desire to understand it, and to determine God's will for his own life, can hardly be faulted. Nor can his general conclusion that "the surest, notablest prognostication of what will befall us is the disposition of our own hearts towards our God...when they are wrong, all goes wrong." For though the righteous may suffer undeservedly, as Johnston himself anticipated, the Bible plainly teaches that backsliding believers can hardly hope to escape some kind of providential chastening.[21] Moreover, Johnston never studied providences in isolation. When seeking guidance on major questions, such as whether his true vocation was to the ministry, he not only remembered his providential preparation in law, but received godly counsel, carefully evaluated his abilities and spent a week in prayer and fasting. What eventually helped him decide, however, was obedience to God's written revelation—"chiefly the warrant of the Apostle commanding me to remain in the calling wherein I was called (1 Corinthians 7:20),"[22] but also other passages, including the parable of the talents.[23] These texts were not randomly selected or twisted to support a prejudice; rather, the decision was reached after much reflection on how the divine precepts applied to this situation.

The Bible was thus, and would remain, the supreme authority

---

20 *Diary, 1655–1660*, 21, 244, 277. See Deuteronomy 29:29; Romans 11:33–34.
21 *Diary, 1632–1639*, 313–314, 307. Compare Hebrews 12:6; Revelation 3:19; 1 Corinthians 11:29–30.
22 *Diary, 1632–1639*, 134–136.
23 Luke 19:12–27.

shaping Johnston's thinking on every subject. Substantial sections of the diary recount his prayerful meditations on the Word encountered through diligent attendance on the means of grace, both public and private. Those who knew him well confirm that he usually rose early and spent "many hours" in "lengthened devotions." One close friend testified that, despite pressure of earthly business, Johnston gave more time to "prayer, meditation and... self-examination than any ever he knew or heard of."[24] Such meditation was not an abstract exercise undertaken out of duty, nor even, primarily, to obtain practical wisdom, but an essential element of the intimate relationship with the living God which constituted the core of his spirituality. At his best, Johnston sought the Lord with a singleminded sincerity that led more frivolous contemporaries to judge him a "very gloomy man." In fact, he enjoyed some precious seasons of "union and communion" with Christ, during which he felt "transported out of [the] body by love, by hope, by joy, and above all by admiration" of the divine goodness. Strong emotions aroused by the sense of God's nearness were sometimes accompanied by bodily manifestations, especially tears and trembling. On one occasion, Johnston even noted that his hair stood on end and "extreme coldness seized on all [his] joints."[25] Strange as these experiences may seem to sceptics in this age of spiritual declension, they are no proof of insanity or fanaticism, and have frequently been reported in times of revival. Compared with fellow Covenanters, Archibald Johnston was far from atypical: his respected colleague and mentor Samuel Rutherford (c.1600–1661), for example, experienced similarly intense rejoicing in the "spring-tide of the

---

24 Gilbert Burnet, Johnston's nephew, cited in George W.T. Omond, *The Lord Advocates of Scotland From the Close of the Fifteenth Century to the Passing of the Reform Bill* (Edinburgh: David Douglas, 1883), 1:149; unnamed friend cited in Robert Wodrow, *The History of the Sufferings of the Church of Scotland from the Restoration to the Revolution* (Glasgow: Blackie, Fullarton, & Co., 1829), 1:361–362.

25 *Diary, 1650–1654*, 195; *Diary, 1632–1639*, 372, 24–25, 251.

consolations of Christ."[26] What prevented subjective ecstasies from degenerating into unorthodox mysticism was the constant correlation between the Spirit's inward influences and contemplation of the objective truths that God has revealed in Scripture.

"That in life and death I might glorify my Lord": *a spirituality of covenant consecration*

The fundamental test of true faith is not fervour but fruitfulness. In Archibald Johnston, experimental knowledge of God's grace soon produced a grateful aspiration "to glorify him, edify...my friends and the poor people," together with a corresponding anxiety "lest the Lord leaving me to myself, I should shame him, scandalize my religion and offend all."[27] Not least among his afflictions, when bereft of his first wife, was despair of doing "any good in the world either by furthering of God's glory, the weal[28] of others, or my own salvation." Yet even in this morbid mental state, "one of [his] greatest worldly wishes" was to "make manifest unto all hearers God's admirable goodness, tender mercies and uncomprehensible kindness" to him. Recovery from depression and remarriage to another godly woman, Helen Hay, redoubled his eagerness and opportunities to bear such witness. As husband, father and master, Johnston not only set an example of personal piety but sought to maintain righteous discipline and supply spiritual as well as material needs. At family worship he "would often pray...two hours at a time." Many of these exercises Johnston recorded in his diaries, which he increasingly hoped would benefit his children.[29]

But Johnston's concern for others was never restricted to his

---

26 *Letters of Samuel Rutherford* (Edinburgh: The Banner of Truth Trust, 1973), 151; compare Yeoman, "Archie's invisible worlds discovered," 163–164, 167.

27 *Diary, 1632–1639*, 364–365.

28 Here used in the now archaic sense to mean "welfare."

29 *Diary, 1632–1639*, 126, 17, 30; Burnet cited in Omond, *Lord Advocates*, 1:149.

immediate household. The decision to "do all the good [he] could do in Christianity without taking on the heavy charge" of a pastor motivated an extensive informal ministry to friends and neighbours, even before the local kirk session appointed him an elder. His prayers and counsel assisted several individuals suffering from sickness or "heavy temptations," including at least one girl with suicidal feelings.[30] Johnston also appreciated the "possibility to serve God and to do good" through assiduity in his "particular calling" to be an advocate. Having commenced by studying Mosaic alongside Scottish law, so as to perceive "the equity and conscionableness of causes," he continued to work in conscious dependence on the Lord, despite receiving "very great applause" from men.[31]

By 1637, Archibald Johnston had reached the peak of personal happiness, enjoying a close walk with God, a flourishing legal practice and a tranquil home with Helen on the small estate at Wariston, lately acquired from her brother. Though thankful for these blessings, he still longed to be a "profitable instrument" in the wider sphere of "church and commonwealth." The events of this year would try the reality of that desire and bring a lasting change to the course of his life. Presbyterianism and patriotism ensured that Johnston could not remain indifferent to the unfolding ecclesiastical and political crisis. But his initial involvement was confined to earnest prayer that the Kirk might not be ruined by reverting to "Romish superstition," organizing local protest against the ritualistic service book imposed by the royal decree of Charles I and expounding that liturgy's "grossest points" to his family. Frustration at these limited opportunities vanished when, to his astonishment, the Scottish nobles leading the opposition nominated him as their advocate. Overwhelmed with delight at "the Lord's deigning to bid me go speak, study, write, plead for himself, his church, his

30 *Diary, 1632–1639*, 152, 348; *Diary, 1650–1654*, 264–266; Yeoman, "Archie's invisible worlds discovered," 178.

31 *Diary, 1632–1639*, 117, 139, 249.

worship—the honourablest, the happiest (albeit the heaviest) charge," Johnston enthusiastically embarked on his new responsibilities, for which he refused any payment. Escalating crisis, due to the king's intransigence, exposed the potential for conflict between public service and private welfare: relatives accurately predicted "that this business would not only crush all my hopes of profit [and] …provision for my children by my calling, but also endanger my present estate…yea, my life and person." Instead of ignoring these warnings, Johnston soberly counted the cost of commitment to the righteous cause, and arrived at "an absolute, free, unreserved, undaunted resolution to take my life and all in my hand, to lay them down at the feet of God." Such entire consecration, regardless of consequences, is the biblical standard for the believer, but has seldom been so unequivocally asserted or solemnly undertaken as it was at this moment in history. Johnston's resolution became the cornerstone of the formal covenants with God that he composed for himself and, with others, for the people of Scotland and England.[32]

If the merits of national covenanting are debatable, the profound, and largely positive influence of these documents on Archibald Johnston is indisputable. Central to his devotional life was his own covenant, renewed eight times by 1653. He warmly commended the practice of "personal formal soul covenanting" to others, especially family members. Meanwhile, fulfilling the public covenants to reform church and state according to God's Word had become his principal political objective, inspiring years of sacrificial service. This overriding determination did not, however, deter him from flexibility as to means. Despite his firm Presbyterian convictions, Johnston was prepared to cooperate with "godly men" of other persuasions, from the Congregationalist John Owen (1616–1683) to the esoteric Henry Vane (1613–1662), in order to promote "good ends." His eventual participation in the Cromwellian and

---

32 *Diary, 1632–1639*, 365, 30, 267, 270–271, 298–299, 281, 306.

republican regimes was much criticized by most of his original colleagues, but surely preferable to the unregenerate Stuart dynasty, which had proved hostile to, and so incompatible with, those primary covenanting aims, "the Glory of God and the Advancement of the Kingdom of our Lord and Saviour Jesus Christ."[33]

Avowed allegiance to his Lord gave Johnston the confidence to confront evil and error in highly placed men—whether monarchs, nobles or Members of Parliament—and the courage to endure impoverishment, exile and, ultimately, execution. Covenants could not, of course, perfect their sinful adherents. On the scaffold in Edinburgh in 1663, Johnston confessed that his actions had sometimes been marred by passionate temper and the intrusion of "self-seeking" motives, and placed all his trust in God's "reconciled Mercy, through the Merits of Jesus Christ." Yet his dying testimony did not repudiate the covenants, but rather glorified God in them, reaffirming the principle of utter submission to God that was such a hallmark of his spirituality.[34]

---

33 *Diary, 1650–1654*, 280, 152–153; *Diary, 1655–1660*, 77–78, 121, 177, 180; A Solemn League and Covenant (1643).

34 *The last discourse of Lord Warestoune*, 5–8.

Chronology

1611
March—Archibald Johnston is born in Edinburgh

1617
April—Johnston's father dies

1626
May—Johnston is converted

1630
Matriculates at Glasgow University

1632
October 23—Johnston marries Jean Stewart

1633
June 6—Jean Stewart dies
July 4—Resolves to record God's dealings with him
August 20—Decides upon a legal career
November 6—Admitted as an Edinburgh advocate

1634
September 4—Johnston marries Helen Hay

1636
Receives charter for estate at Wariston from his
brother-in-law Alexander Hay

1637
July 23—Riot in Edinburgh against the imposition

of the service book: start of Scottish resistance to Charles I
October 17—Johnston presents supplication against the service
book on behalf of his local kirk session
November 20—Johnston is approached by national
opposition leaders
December 5—Johnston accepts nomination to act as advocate
on behalf of the Scottish nobles

1638

February 23—Johnston is asked to draft the document that
became the National Covenant
April 1—National Covenant is publically adopted in Edinburgh
May 26—Johnston is appointed an elder by the
Currie kirk session
November 21—Johnston is appointed clerk to the general
assembly of the Kirk meeting in Glasgow
December—Johnston is appointed procurator of the Kirk

1639

June—Johnston is a commissioner negotiating the Pacification
of Berwick, which ends the First Bishops' war between the
Covenanters and Charles I

1640

June—Johnston is appointed to the Committee of Estates
ruling Scotland
July–September—Second Bishops' war: the king is defeated at
Newburn; the Scots occupy Newcastle
October—Assists in negotiating Treaty of Ripon which
suspends hostilities; travels to London
November 3—Opening of the Long Parliament in London

1641

August—Charles I concedes most of the Covenanters' demands
September—Scottish Parliament acknowledges
Johnston's loyal service
November 13—Johnston is knighted and made a judge in the
court of session, with the honorary title Lord Wariston

1642

August 2—The Civil War begins in England

1643

June—Johnston is elected MP for Midlothian,
County Edinburgh
August—Johnston persuades Scots to support the English
Parliament: negotiates the Solemn League and Covenant;
Johnston is nominated to the Westminster Assembly

1644

January—Johnston is appointed to the Committe of Both
Kingdoms directing the joint war effort from London
July 2—Victory of the Parliamentary and Scottish forces
at Marston Moor
September—Outbreak of Montrose's rebellion against the
Covenanting regime in Scotland

1645

June 10—Parliamentary victory at Naseby
September—Montrose is defeated; Johnston successfully
advocates severe punishment of Montrose's supporters

1646

March—Johnston gives a speech against Erastianism at the
Westminster Assembly

May—Charles I surrends to the Scots, ending the
first phase of the Civil War
November—Johnston is appointed King's Advocate

1647
January—The Scots relinquish Charles I to the English
Parliament and withdraw
December—Secret Engagement treaty between Charles and
Scots commissioners

1648
March—Disclosure of Engagement terms split the Covenanters;
Johnston vigorously but unsuccessfully opposes the treaty;
Johnston contemplates emigration
Outbreak of the Second Civil War
August 17—Oliver Cromwell defeats the Scots at the
Battle of Preston; Johnston's faction, the Kirk party,
take control of Scotland

1649
January—The trial and execution of Charles I
Johnston is MP for Argyllshire in new Scottish Parliament:
prepares Act of Classes disqualifying Engagers from
public office
February 6—Scots conditionally proclaim Charles II
king of Great Britain
March 10—Johnston appointed Clerk Register, with custody of
Scotland's records

1650
June—Treaty of Heligoland between Charles II and Kirk party:
king takes covenants to secure admission to Scotland

September 3—Cromwell's victory at the Battle of Dunbar
deprives the Kirk party of power
October—Covenanters are divided between the minority
Remonstrants, including Johnston, who opposed further aid to
Charles II unless he sincerely repented, and the majority
Resolutioners, so called for their support of the Scottish
Parliament's resolutions against the Remonstrance

1651
September 3—Victory for Cromwell at the Battle of Worcester.
End of the Civil Wars

1652
April—English Parliament's resolve to unite Scotland with
England proclaimed at Edinburgh
Johnston refuses to cooperate with the conquerors and
retires to private life

1653
December 12—Cromwell becomes Lord Protector

1657
June—Johnston travels to London on behalf of
the Remonstrant party
July 9—Johnston is reappointed Clerk Register by Cromwell
November 3—Johnston is appointed as a commissioner for the
administration of justice in Scotland

1658
January—Johnston is nominated by Cromwell to the new
Other House of the British Parliament
September 3—Death of Oliver Cromwell, whose son Richard
succeeds him as Lord Protector

1659

January—Johnston takes his seat in the Other House
of Richard's Parliament
April—Fall of Richard Cromwell
May—English army restore the republic under the Long
Parliament, which call Johnston to the Council of State
June 3—Johnston first presides in Council
October 13—Army coup against Parliament:
Johnston's mediation averts bloodshed
October 22—Officers name Johnston to the new executive
Committee of Safety, where he again presides
December 26—Parliament restored following the collapse
of the Committee and the English army; power passes to
General Monck and the army in Scotland

1660

January—Johnston goes into hiding in London
March 16—The Long Parliament dissolves itself
May—Restoration of Charles II
July—Warrant for Johnston's arrest is issued
October—Johnston escapes to the Continent

1661

February 2—Johnston summoned to answer treason charge,
excepted from Indemnity Act
May 13—Johnston is sentenced to death *in absentia*;
his estates are forfeited

1662

December—Johnston is betrayed and
arrested in France

1663

January—Johnston is extradited to England, imprisoned and interrogated in the Tower of London

June—Johnston is transferred to the Tolbooth in Edinburgh

July 8—Johnston appears before the Scottish Parliament who confirm his death sentence

July 23—Johnston is hanged and decapitated at the Mercat Cross, Edinburgh

Archibald Johnston of Wariston

Selections from his diaries and speeches

1

Opening of "Memento Quamdiu Vivas" [1]

1633

O most gracious God, and to me ever a most merciful in forgiving and a most indulgent Father in giving more nor ever my heart could desire;

As thou hast oft grieved my soul unto the very death by presenting unto my memory the doleful catalogue of my abominable works, words and thoughts...since ever I knew good or evil—which sight ever made my knees to smite one against another, as Belshazzar's at the sight of *mene mene tekel*, and rent my heart as Hezekiah his clothes at the hearing of Rabshaketh's blasphemies;[2] and on the other part, as thou hast oft comforted me not only by pacifying the cries of an accusing Satan, a condemning conscience, and an executing vengeance, by the louder cry of that blood which cries

---

1 G.M. Paul, ed., *The Diary of Sir Archibald Johnston of Wariston, 1632–1639* (Edinburgh: Scottish History Society, 1911), 1. The Latin phrase means, "Remember as long as you live."

2 Daniel 5:6; Isaiah 37:1.

for better things nor the blood of Abel,[3] but also hast overjoyed my heart by making me see the catalogue of thy bygone mercies, indulgent to me above all admiration by turning all that befell me unto my manifest weal[4] by a special overruling providence, whereof all the footsteps ever dropped fatness unto me, and ever made my cup to overflow.[5] So now, O Father, my soul, whom thou hast oft dejected and oft comforted, beggeth, craveth instantly and humbly, at thy fatherly kindness through the merits of the Lord Jesus, that thou wouldst open my eyes for to see and sanctify my memory for to remember all the footsteps of thy fatherly wrath in casting me down by this cross[6] of thy fatherly love, in assisting me under it, and delivering me from it, that this experience of thy favour may strengthen my faith in the day of new troubles, and that through Christ Jesus, to whom with the Father and Holy Ghost be all praise.

---

3 Hebrews 12:24
4 Meaning "welfare."
5 Compare Psalm 65:11; 23:5.
6 The death of his first wife, Jean Stewart, on June 6, 1633.

2

The road to matrimony [1]

1626-1632

My soul, never forget, but ever remember to God's glory and thy comfort, how in the sixteenth year of thy age, in the months of May and June, whilst thou was a Latiner, [2] God dealt wonderfully with thee principally at the communion of the Pans [3] ...and continually every evening and morning in thy mother's gallery. [4] Also how, after thou went unto France, all the three months of August, September and October: and after thou camest home...until thy marriage: remember...the days of old, and how sensible in them thou wast both of thy own misery and of God's mercy: how by the sight of the one thou hast been thrown down in the lower hells, and by the sense of the other thou hast been lifted up unto the highest heaven....

Meditate on those last three months, wherein God was dealing with thee before thy marriage and preparing thee for a blessing:

---

1   *Diary, 1632–1639*, 1–3.
2   Meaning "a Latin scholar."
3   Prestonpans, Scotland.
4   Meaning "room."

how God held thee ever waking, either by the sight of thy sins, or, these [having] been washed away to thy sense in the blood of the Lamb, by the continual buffets of Satan and fears to yield to the temptation: how thou out of thy agony hast sensibly cried, "O miserable captive that I am, who shall deliver me from this body of death?"[5]

[Remember] how the spirit of prayer was poured out on thee, and this alternative ever in thy mouth, "Lord, either keep me from being tempted; or, in the temptation, let me find thy renewing grace sufficient for me, as I have oft found thy restraining grace provident; or grant me liberty to use and bless me in the use of a lawful remedy, to wit in my marriage."

O my soul, remember that, when neither finding God preserving thee from the temptation, nor in it…thou resolved, by God's help to be married…what perplexities, what fears overwhelmed thee. Thou wist[6] not whom to choose, yea thou durst not trust thyself nor thy friends…for thou knewest thyself might be deceived by thy passion for a fair face, and they for a great dowry. At last, having obtained the guilt of my bygone ill affections…pardoned in the blood of the Lord Jesus, I disburdened myself of all those thoughts, doubts, and cares, and laid them on the Lord Jesus who bears all our burdens,[7] and cried to thee, O God, being reconciled with Jehosaphat, "I know not what to do, but my eyes are upon thee."[8]

How oft, my soul, hast thou told the Lord that he loved thee better than thy friends nor thou did thyself: he knew better than they or thou what was fittest for his glory and thy weal;[9] he was also powerfuller than they or thou to bring to pass what out of his love he thought good for thee, and so…I was forced to burden him

---

5 Romans 7:24.
6 An obsolete verb meaning "to know."
7 See 1 Peter 5:7; Psalm 55:22.
8 2 Chronicles 20:12.
9 Meaning "welfare."

with this care, being fully persuaded that God the Father who had not spared his only begotten Son for my cause,[10] and God the Son who had not spared his own body, life and soul, and God the Holy Ghost who had lodged in my heart so long and assured me of all their favours—they three being the makers of my marriage—that come what would come I should find, and all the world with me should see…God's extraordinary indulgence and provident carefulness to bless me visibly in that marriage…. Only on this goodness of God did my soul rely.

---

10 See Romans 8:32.

3

Marriage to Jean Stewart[1]

1632-1633

O soul, remember on Wednesday morning thou rose by two hours,[2] and was continually crying to the Lord that he would bless thee that day with the greatest of his worldly blessings. Having read Genesis 24 about God's prospering Abraham's servant in his obtaining Rebekah to wife for Isaac, thou craved that he would let thee see his providence in the bringing it about, and his indulgence to thee and her in perfecting it.... Never forget how about five hours in the morning...thou humbly, fervently and confidently invited God thy Father, Christ thy elder brother, and the Holy Ghost thy old guest, as...thy nearest, dearest friends...unto the marriage, praying...that God the Father would bless the bride and bridegroom with love first to him and then to one another, that Christ my elder brother would rain down all his graces on us both, and that the Holy Ghost...would bring all his spiritual consolations and

---

1 *Diary, 1632–1639*, 9–11.
2 i.e. 2 a.m. on the wedding day.

promises to remain with her and with me for ever. Remember how confidently, with tears running over thy cheeks like water, thou blessed God the Father, the Son and the Holy Ghost for all their bygone favours and for the assurance they gave…that they were the makers of the marriage and…would turn it unto…their own glory… the salvation of her and thy soul…. So praying God and trusting in God thou was married October 23, 1632….

Remember thereafter on Sunday night when thou went home to thy own house thou said the prayer and dedicated therein thyself, thy wife and thy family unto God's service, and ever after, morning and evening, thou said the prayer after some meditation as God furnished thee conceptions and words by his Spirit. Remember… how often God has made thee speak to her of God and godliness in thy bed, and to pass over all the principles of religion…. Remember how thy heart was ravished with her answers, and blessed God for her. Remember when God moved thee extraordinarily…to call upon her and both together humbly to confess our sins, cry for pardon and ask a blessing upon us both. Remember all the winter mornings sometimes you expounded your Greek chapter to her, sometimes she got two Psalms every morning and repeated them to you, sometimes she read the Bible in her bed….

4

Bereavement and despondency[1]

June 1633

On June 12, 1633…it pleased God upon a sudden, for causes known to himself, to separate those souls which he had joined out of his love, and to take the one to eternal glory, and to leave the other plunged in an unspeakable misery…. O the suddenness of it confounds me yet; but…when I remembered who had done [it], even the Lord, even my Father, even he who gave me her…. O soul, thy sorrow passed all compassion when thou called to mind how… in the perfecting of that match, the Lord had visibly let thee see his hearing of thy prayer and his admirable love…yet the same God had now…cast thee loose again to the jaws of temptation and had taken away…all those blessings which thou hadst prayed for, he had promised…and had given…. The remembrance of the days of old, of God's bygone love turned to present wrath for my abominations, and the foresight of a miserable, sinful and doleful life was ever in

---

1   *Diary, 1632–1639*, 13, 15–17.

my sight and galled my soul with terrors, sorrow and fears....

I never thought on her without comfort, in respect of my assurance she was with the Lord and my good conscience that I had striven, both in exhortations to godliness unto herself and by fervent prayers unto the Lord to increase the fear of God and love of godliness in her heart, whereof I had seen so many signs.... When I looked to the affliction itself, I found my heart speaking with Job, "God gave me her, he has taken her back; blessed be his name"[2] ...I was even content to quit my right of her unto the Lord for her eternal happiness, seeing I loved her so well that I would prefer her enjoying of that heavenly bliss to all my worldly contentment in her.

I never had any hope, or very little (except trusting in God's absolute power) to do any good in the world either by furthering of God's glory, the weal[3] of others, or my own salvation, in private life of a Christian or in the public one of a particular calling. First because I never found no ability for the last...on the contrary I found God ever crossing my studies when I set my mind to use the ordinary means for the enabling me therein, and for the doing any good in the calling of a Christian, now God has taken away the occasion of it by separating my family...and calling to himself my wife, to whom I was ever communicating the good that God did to my soul.

---

2 Job 1:21.
3 Meaning "welfare."

5

Resting in God's reconciliation[1]

June 30, 1633

O my soul, remember that Sunday...after the sermon...how God moved thee to reckon over...all thy sins committed since thy marriage, and parallelling thy life of those bygone seven months with the ten commandments and finding thyself guilty a thousand-fold of them all, and not only by sinning against God's precepts but against his mercies....All my sins...crying for vengeance, the devil accusing me of far more...the very fear drowned me, and God seeming to hear their cries and having begun to inflict his punishments...the fear of greater judgements so confounded my soul as never any of God's children was nearer to be drowned in the pit of desperation.... But my extremity was the Lord's opportunity, for then the Spirit of God began to cry in me with those sighs and sobs inexpressible; then Christ, audibly and visibly to the eyes and ears of my soul, began to intercede for me; then the Father said to my soul, "Be of good comfort, thy sins are forgiven...and seeing I

---

1 *Diary, 1632–1639*, 19–20.

45

am reconciled to thee, thou may be assured I will provide for all the rest to my own glory and thy comfort."[2]

Remember, O soul, what ease thou then found in thy troubles, and how the cross of Christ sweetened the bitterness of all thy crosses.

---

2 Compare Romans 8: 26,34,32.

6

Resolving to remember [1]

July 4, 1633

Remember on Thursday morning while thou prayed, meditating on Psalm 50:15, "Call upon me in the day of trouble: I will deliver thee and thou shalt glorify me," how assured thou wast of God's delivering thee both from the burden of affliction and temptation in his own time, since he enabled thee to do thy part to call on him, yea that Christ Jesus, before the Father and the Holy Spirit in me called for me, he would the rather perform his own part, yea not only he gave thee grace to call on him in prayer but he moved thee to call on him before thy ordinary time when he saw any occasion was to divert at that time. And there, soul, while thou was on thy knees, assuredly as if thou had already been delivered, thou fell to glorifying God and vowed there to the Lord, first, to remark all the footsteps of his providence, either in casting me down or lifting me up; and secondly to remark and bless the Lord all the days of my lifetime every morning and evening, particularly for the particular delivery of my soul from this present burden of

---

1   *Diary, 1632–1639*, 21–22.

affliction and temptation, as one day my soul hopeth confidently for to do it.

7

Repentance and rejoicing [1]

July 8, 1633

O heavens, O earth, O angels and saints, O all ye works of his hands, come, concur, and help my soul to sing aloud hallelujah, praise, honour and glory to God the Father, God the Son and God the Holy Ghost! For this morning…my soul being oppressed with grief and distracted with fears, happened by God's providence to read Joel 2:12–14. But before thou read it, remember, my soul, how thou humbled thyself before the Lord, begging instantly from his mercy that he would…speak one word of reconciliation to thy broken heart, and one word of consolation to thy afflicted soul, and one word of direction to thy irresolved mind. Thereafter, remember how at the reading ("therefore saith the Lord") thou roused up thyself to hear what the Lord had to say, and ("Turn ye even to me with all thy heart, and with fasting and weeping and mourning") how thou answered, "Lord, thou hast turned all my heart already; all my heart, yea all the affections thereof, all my desires long for

1 *Diary, 1632–1639,* 22–25.

thee, all my joy is in thy presence, yea all my grief is not so much for being deprived of all worldly contentment...as for the sake of thy wrath kindled by my guiltiness clearly appearing."[2] ...

O my soul, and all the faculties thereof, O my heart and all the affections thereof, O my body and all the members thereof, sing honour, praise and glory to God the Father, the Son and the Holy Ghost, when thou remember how God said to thee, "I see thou hast turned to me with all thy heart, and that thou hast rent it out of grief for the offending of me; as thou hast repented of the evil of sin, so I will let thee see I repent me of the evil of punishment whereby I have afflicted thee and that I will leave a blessing.... Look now, O my son reconciled...on the heavens and on the earth and on all that therein is...and choose anything contained therein... I will deny you nothing, but will grant it as a sign...of my reconciliation to you."[3] ...

O soul, can man or angel express how thou wast transported out of thy body by love, by hope, by joy, and above all by admiration; how trembled thy body...thou fell down on thy knees and said that this ravishing of thy soul with the praises of his goodness was a sufficient sign...thou asked only a broken and a contrite heart that thou mayst pour it out like water before him.... Then the Lord sware that as he lived he would give me it, and seeing I had sought first the kingdom of heaven that he would cast all other things in my lap, and with himself give me all.[4]

Now, my soul...remember...how thereafter all thy prayers were turned unto praises.

---

2 A positive application of Joel 2:13–14.

3 Compare Psalm 51:17; 62:8.

4 Matthew 6:33; Proverbs 16:33; Romans 8:32.

8

Wrestling in prayer [1]

July 10, 13 & 15, 1633

Remember how on Wednesday morning God brought that thought in thy head, "The prayer of the faithful prevaileth much" [2] if it be fervent.

To make thy prayer fervent, thou meditated on the necessity of it, and to make it faithful on the experience of God's bygone delivery and his promises....When thou began to reflect...on thyself...thou found a necessity commanding thee to cry aloud, when thou considered God's blessings ever multiplied on thee, "Praise, honour and glory unto the giver;" when thou considered thy unthankfulness... and abuse of them, "Mercy and pardon in the blood of the Lord Jesus for his love sake." ...Here, soul, being oppressed with the sight of thy bygone sins, present affliction and future temptation, thou turned all into one prayer, using David's arguments in Psalm 25 for thy deliverance from all three—as at verse 11, "Pardon my iniquity,

---

1 *Diary, 1632–1639*, 26–30.
2 James 5:16.

O Lord, for it is great," at verse 16, "Have mercy on me, for I am desolate and afflicted" and at verse 20, "Let me not be ashamed, for I put my trust in thee."

Saturday morning found thee…oppressed with grief and almost at the brink of desperation…until thou read the hindmost three verses of Matthew 11 ("Come unto me, all ye that are weary and laden, and I will relieve you," etc.). Here thy conscience bearing the witness of thy…bygone sins, of God's present wrath and the temptations of my flesh, which every hour thou fears will swallow thee…and on the other part God commanding me to come and promising me relief, yea and my experience of relief bygone… encouraged me to fall down on my knees and thank him for his bygone deliverances and instantly crave that either he would relieve me according to his promise…or that he would assure me of reconciliation…and enable me to resist the temptation; and that he would be pleased in his own time to deliver me out of them all, either by calling my soul out of this valley of tears…unto life everlasting where my other half blesses him eternally, or by making me in my life not to scandalize his religion and my profession, but rather to further his glory….

Remember, my soul, in the old kirk[3] before sermon forenoon, how all thy hopes were laid in the dust and thy heart pitifully dejected at the singing of Psalm 23 when thou called to memory the days of old in which thou hadst so cheerfully sung that psalm, and chiefly that verse, "My cup doth overflow,"[4] which thou now sawest at so low an ebb either of spiritual or worldly comforts…. But by God's providence the afternoon text was Psalm 103, "Bless the Lord, O my soul: who forgiveth all thine iniquities and healeth all thy diseases."[5]…Thou prayed the Lord first that, seeing thou knew not whether death or life was ordained for thee he would

---

3 This is a Scottish word for "church."
4 Psalm 23:5.
5 Psalm 103:2–3.

make thee indifferent to both…. Second, that if he was to put an end to thy miseries presently, he would prepare thy mind to glorify him and edify his saints the better in the hour of thy death, and so would permit thee to confess thy own natural misery ever fighting against God in all thy lifetime, and to make manifest unto all hearers God's admirable goodness, tender mercies and uncomprehensible kindness to thee in all that ever befell—"and O Lord, thou knowest this is one of my greatest worldly wishes, to manifest this to thy world ere I die." Or, if he was to continue my days in the world, he would enable me with those graces that may keep me from shaming of him…and would endue me with those parts and gifts as are necessary to further his glory, the weal[6] of the church and commonwealth, and my own salvation.

---

6 Meaning "welfare."

9

Dependence despite the darkness [1]

July 16 & 22, 1633

On Monday at night…thou called to mind how God…had blessed thee in giving thee thy wife and…taken her…to let thee see his special hand and providence both in giving thee any good or sending thee any evil, that thou may acknowledge every good gift to descend from above, and every evil in the city to be done by the Lord;[2] and learn also to depend on him alone, never to distrust him or to trust in any other thing. And thereafter, having cast my eyes on my present estate and seeing no appearance nor shadow of appearance of deliverance, yea nature, grace and godliness abhorring now the means whereby God delivered me from temptation before, my soul was almost desperate, if I had not considered this to be God's ordinary dealing with his own, and not daring to mistrust either his power or his good will, seeing he had given

---

1   *Diary, 1632–1639*, 32, 55.
2   See James 1:17; Amos 3:6.

himself to be my portion. I remembered my case to be like that of Jehosophat's, "We know not what to do, but our eyes are upon the Lord,"[3] and so hoped above hope, contrary to all appearance, for that answer he received from the Lord…and like to those of Psalm 22:5: "Our fathers cried unto thee, O Lord, and were delivered: they trusted in thee and were not confounded." My soul cries as they did, "Let me therefore be delivered; my soul trusts in thee as they did, let me not therefore be confounded. But O Lord, purge me now, in the fire of affliction, from the dross of my inward corruption."[4]

On the Tuesday morning, having prayed to God that, seeing I trusted in him, hoped for him, and prayed to him, he would not disappoint my trust, frustrate my hopes nor reject the prayer of a contrite heart, then I turned Psalm 120 into a meditation. Verse 1, "In my distress I cried unto the Lord, and he heard me." Verse 5, "Woe unto me that I sojourn in Mesech" (of a sinful world) "and that I dwell in the tents of Kedar" (of my abominable body); and also Psalm 121:1, "I will lift up my eyes unto the hills" (yea, unto the cross of Christ on Mount Calvary) "from whence cometh my help? My help cometh from the Lord"; verse 7, "The Lord shall preserve thee from all evil"…Lord Jesus, preserve me from sin, and do with me what thou wilt.

---

3 2 Chronicles 20:12.
4 Compare Malachi 3:2–3; Isaiah 48:10; 1 Peter 1:7.

10

Usefulness of recorded memories in adversity [1]

July 22, 1633

I began to read my own papers concerning God's dealing with me before my marriage, and there first I was more than ever dejected, almost desperately if God secretly had not upheld me. Thereafter, at the sight of every particular I was forced with many tears of joy and sorrow to fall down and to bless God the Father, Son and Holy Ghost for their love towards me…and to pray them instantly to manifest the like love to me now in the day of my greater necessity….

Now soul, never forget how oft thou wast on thy knees blessing God so heartily and praying to him so instantly to continue the same God, as loving, as indulgent, as merciful, as provident, as tenderly kind, to thee now in the day of thy unutterable extremity as ever he had been to thee before; vowing unto the Lord, if he would deal so bountifully with thee his unworthy servant, that thy soul

---

1 *Diary, 1632–1639*, 56–57.

and all thy faculties.. should ever honour, bless and praise his goodness.[2]

...Never forget with what innumerable tears and unexpressible sighs and troubled mind thou confessed unto the Lord particularly all thy sins against his merciful love since thy marriage.... O how was thy conscience wakened and thy heart poured out, running unto the Father in the mediation of the Lord Jesus who came only in the world to save penitent sinners of whom I am the greatest.[3]

---

2 Compare Psalm 119:17; 142:7.
3 Compare 1 Timothy 2:5; 1:15.

11

Desperation [1]

July 23-24, 1633

O soul remember, thou being ever mindful of that maxim, "Mans extremity is God's opportunity," on Tuesday afternoon thou cried, "Now, Lord, I am come to an extremity." But on Wednesday morning, thou cried, "O Lord, woe now is, my griefs grow and multiply." [Then] at eleven, in thy extreme agony, thou shouted, "O Lord, never was my soul in hell before now: my God, my God, why forsakest thou me now when heaven and hell, the earth, my own conscience and all is conspiring my ruin? In all Psalm 107 never one of thy saints was in the perplexity that I am in; my soul fails me, my heart faints, my spirits are overwhelmed, I draw near unto the gates of death.[2] ...Yet do I cry, trusting in the merits of the Lamb of God that takes away the sins of poor, penitent captives, of whom I am the most miserable and so the fittest object of his mercy, the most desperately diseased and so the fittest patient...the most laden

---

1 *Diary, 1632–1639*, 58–59.
2 Compare Psalm 22:1; Song of Songs 5:6; Psalm 77:3,26; 143:4; 107:18.

and wearied soul that lives; therefore Lord have mercy, cure and relieve, for now I am at the brink of despair.[3]

Yet, O soul, never forget how in this extremity of grief thou confessed thy sins and craved pardon of them in God's well-beloved. …I foretell…the remembrance of this godly sorrow may one day comfort thee in the day of trouble and uphold thee in the day of temptation.[4]…O soul, bless God…and hope in God reconciled for a deliverance, and as thou repentest of the evil of sin, so [hope] that he will repent him of the evil of punishment.[5]

---

3 Compare John 1:29; Romans 7:23–24; Matthew 11:28.
4 2 Corinthians 7:10.
5 See Jonah 3:10.

12

Assurance of salvation: the Scheins experience [1]

July 27, 1633

Saturday morning…in the Scheins long alley, my soul ever remember to God's glory and thy comfort, when thou entered the alley how earnestly thou prayed that God would be pleased that morning to speak reconciliation, consolation and direction unto thy guilty, afflicted, confounded soul…. Having begged this again from him in the mediation of Christ, thou vowed, being suddenly moved by God's Spirit, that if he would deal so mercifully with his unworthy servant now, that thy soul, thy heart and thy body should bless and praise him extraordinarily for it. Even before thou went out of that alley the very making of this vow…made thy mind even then, when thou saw no appearance of it, yet to presage[2]…that God was to comfort thee one way or other that morning as he did indeed, and therefore again my soul, remember his goodness in writing it

---

1 *Diary, 1632–1639*, 63–66.
2 Meaning to "foreshadow."

down…. Calling to mind how often…I had confessed particularly, mourned unutterably, and cried for pardon in the blood of Christ most ardently, and now had amended all those same sins in some measure, I was forced on a sudden to fall down on my knees and to bless God for those tears of godly sorrow, and to praise God's goodness for them, and comfort myself by them, as by many signs of my remission and God's reconciliation. Then remembering my vow at my entry to the alley, again I was forced to sing hallelujah to God the Father for his love in pardoning, to God the Son for his love in dying meriting my pardon, and to the Holy Spirit for his love in groaning for me to the Father and assuring me of God's free love and gracious mercy pardoning all in the blood of his well-beloved Son, my Lord. Soul, never remember or read this but sing honour, praise and glory to them all three eternally….

O soul, never forget…how then the assurance of thy reconcilation, and thereby thy hope now to be shortly delivered from all thy miseries, made all thy body…to quake, tremble and coldly to shake…. Then, O soul, with what ease of mind and confidence in God reconciled went thou to him…even confidently to put up this petition unto him…."O loving Father, reconciled in Christ, I being but sinful dust…having ever before my eyes my bygone stubborn ungrateful sinning against thy lovingkindness…I durst not…present this petition unto thee, if my recent experience, first of thy granting me a contrite heart, and now a conscience pacified by the sense of thy reconciliation, and some inward…motion of thy Spirit forcing me to seek this…that thou would so turn my present troubles and my delivery from them to so visible a glorification of thy name…and to so sensible a consolation and salvation of my soul as that, with me, all that saw me cast down should see thee raise me up….Lord… pardon once, as thou did Abraham's,[3] my boldness; and seeing thou forced me to pray for it, hasten thou to hear and perform it."

---

3 Genesis 18:23–32.

13

Consolation through the means of grace: the Word preached [1]

July 28, 1633

On Sunday morning, not finding thy heart at the beginning so soft as it used to be, thou wast almost confounded, fearing lest yesterday's assurance of reconciliation should cast thee into a security, impenitence and hardness of heart. But then bitterly, yet confusedly, thou cried, "O Lord, this is the misery of miseries, when I got a heart to cry thou hadst not an ear to hear (yet thou heardst me at last, blessed be thy name...) and now when thou art reconciled and...ready for to hear, I have not a heart to cry; this thy not permitting my praying and thy hearing to concur may be a sure token that thou art not minded to deliver or to bless me." But thereafter I remembered one of Mr. Henry Rollock's[2] sermons during my prosperity about... how we should use God's blessings thankfully, charitably, moderately.... Looking about me and seeing

---

1 *Diary, 1632–1639,* 69–70, 72–75.
2 An Edinburgh minister whom Johnston often heard preach.

myself stripped naked of all those blessings which I then enjoyed, and reflecting…upon my own guiltiness procuring this change… then, indeed, I began to howl, mourn and lament with many tears to my great content, desiring the Lord above all things to continue with me a broken heart and a contrite spirit, and vowing…that if he would deal so indulgently with his distressed servant and would now in his sanctuary…speak some comfort to thy wearied heart, that then…thou wouldst greatly magnify his goodness.[3]

My soul, bless God for moving thee to put up this petition, and then for his…granting it unto thee beyond thy expectation. For afternoon Mr. Archibald Scaldee[4] preached most comfortably for me on Psalm 145:14: "The Lord upholdeth all that fall and raiseth up all those that be bowed down." The very reading of the text made thee presage[5] some notable comfort…for which thou blessed God before he began…. He made two expositions…. Out of the first he said, "God upholds those that fall in sin, first by keeping them from committing it, and that by removing all the occasions of it and temptations out of the way, or by not suffering them to concur," and here, soul, thou blessed God for thy own experience of God's keeping thee wonderfully from the tyranny and scandalous acts of lust in thy youth. Secondly, God suffered his own dearest children to fall unto gross sins for four causes:

First, to glorify himself in his mercy the more, for without sin no misery and misery is the only object of mercy, "O Lord," cried I, "then am I most miserable and so the fittest object of thy mercy."

Second, for to teach them humility, which is the mother and nurse of all other spiritual graces.

Third, to make them more circumspect in their ways both in foreseeing the occasions and in more resisting the temptation.

---

3 Psalm 34:18.
4 The blind preacher in the college kirk, Edinburgh.
5 Meaning to "foreshadow."

Fourth, to make them contemn more and more the world, wherein they are compassed so about with outward temptations, inward corruptions, multitude of evil examples…and to allure their hearts the more with the love of that heavenly inheritance wherein they will never be sinning, but ever singing and praising God's mercy for pardoning their iniquities and ending their miseries. O here my soul cried, "Lord, I take thee to witness my soul groaneth, longeth, panteth to be out of this body of death…and to be with thee…it is my desire and wish all the hours of the day and of the night. Lord thou canst, and I hope thou wilt, perfect it in thy own time…come Lord Jesus, for welcome and long looked for art thou."[6]…

The second exposition was, "The Lord upholds those that fall unto trouble and affliction."

First, by preserving them from trouble wherein they see their neighbours, perhaps better Christians, almost drowned…wherefore we should learn in…prosperity to bless God for it, to pray…for the continuance thereof and granting the right use of it.

Second, by comforting them under it with the sense of his presence and the testimony of a good conscience that they love, desire and long for him…more than…anything. (Here, soul, thou remembered and blessed God for thy rejoicing under thy manifold troubles…)

Third, by delivering them finally from their trouble while they are bowed down under the sense of it. And if any, said he, would be delivered that way, let him do three things:

1. Be sensible of his cross and humbled under it; and then, ascending to his sins the procurers of it, let him be above all sensible of them, confess them to God, mourn for them, crave pardon in the blood of the Lamb and strive to amend.
2. With David, let him humbly…cry Psalm 119:49, "Re-

---

6 Romans 8:23; 7:24; Psalm 38:9–10; 42:1.

member, O Lord, thy word…unto thy servant, upon which thou hast caused me to hope."

3. Trust only, only in the Lord crying with Jehosaphat, "I know not what to do, but my eyes are upon thee, O Lord," and assuredly, said he, you shall find the answer that came unto Jehosaphat, "Stand still and see the salvation of the Lord."[7]

Remember then, O soul, how thy heart was notably comforted by the testimony of thy conscience…that I had in some measure… performed these three duties, so…that I was forced to bless God for granting…my morning vow and afternoon prayer.

---

7 2 Chronicles 20:17.

14

Consolation through the means of grace: communion and its aftermath[1]

August 5-7, 1633

Now my soul, to God's glory and thy comfort, ever remember how extraordinarily God moved thee when thou went to the table, how in going in thou ejaculated, out of the unutterable grief of thy soul, "Now Father, here [is] thy prodigal son, here is the publican, here is a sinful, doleful, confounded soul: pardon, pity and deliver. Father, be now a Father; Christ, be now a Saviour; Holy Spirit, be now a comforter; pardon, pity, deliver." When thou was sitting at the table, soul, never forget how thy whole body trembled...and pained thee with pain out of an excessive ardour wherewith thou prayed to the Almighty, how thy heart was poured out before God in innumerable tears and inexpressible groans. Then the minister seeing thee so moved, for thou sat next him, he began his exhortation with

---

1   *Diary, 1632–1639*, 96–100.

Matthew 11:28: "Come unto me, all ye that are weary and laden, and I will relieve you." O soul, struck not these words at thy heart, and confounded thee with admiration of God's goodness making him choose a passage so fit for thy present estate? ...Not waiting whether to praise or to pray, but having blessed him thou cried, "O God, I, an unworthy worm,[2] dare attest my conscience that I am laden and weary under the burden of my guiltiness, thy wrath and of my present confusion, and...of my very life:[3] Father, Saviour, Comforter, therefore pardon, pity, deliver." At the taking of the cup both thy head and hand so tottered and trembled as almost thou could not drink.... Never forget how after the drinking and blessing of God, thy very soul cried within thee, "Now, Father, lettest thou thy servant depart in peace; for my eyes have seen thy salvation."[4]

Soul, remember God never so prepared thee for a communion; never so moved thee at one; and therefore hope that thou shalt one day reap greater comfort thereby than thou knowest yet. Thereafter thou cried, "Now, Lord, remember the word whereon thou hast made thy servant for to hope."[5]

The exhortation following was about our new covenant, which on God's part was grace and glory; on our part, faith and obedience; ...having blessed God for calling thee to this communion, preparing thee for it, and comforting thee...at it, thou heard the thanksgiving upon Psalm 50:23, "Whoso offereth praise glorifieth me, and to him that ordereth his conversation aright will I show the salvation of God." After sermon, in my own chamber, having prayed...for a contrite heart, I got my very soul humbly, instantly and confidently poured out before God in an unspeakable manner and measure, yea even with greater confidence, humility and instance than ever in my lifetime; which comforted me extraordinarily, seeing God then

---

2 Compare Psalm 22:6.
3 Compare Job 10:1.
4 Luke 2:29.
5 Psalm 119:49.

teaching me to pray when he…was assuredly readiest for to hear….

On Monday night…never forget…that God admirably began to comfort thee by spreading the sense of his love in the death of Christ abroad in thy heart;[6] then, first he assured thee that he had relieved thee at this communion from thy first and greatest burden…thy guiltiness, which is the cause of all the rest. Thereafter he distilled comfort in thy heart against thy second burden of seeing his wrath in the recalling of his blessings, arguing against thyself that now the sight of his love and unspeakable mercy in the giving of his only begotten Son unto the ignominious death of the cross for thy sake[7]…should counterbalance the sight of his wrath in recalling thy wife. The first should comfort thee more than the other deject thee, because the first is a most assured…sign of a superabundant, superincomprehensible love to thee, and the second is but a… doubtful token of a little wrath,[8] yea only of a fatherly correction, so that thy joy in the mercies of God should exceed thy grief for present miseries, since thou couldst not question the power of God nor doubt his love, which the Father manifested in not sparing his only begotten Son, and the Son showed in shedding his own heart's blood for thee.[9]

And suppose thou doubted his love, yet thou durst not doubt the infallibility of his promises, which now he must perform for his own name's sake, and so thou mightst be assured of a final and total deliverance from all thy troubles in God's own time. Then thy soul being filled with love of God and hope of thy deliverance rejoiced unspeakably in the Lord, remembering that passage, "Ask, and receive, that your joy may be full,"[10] and how often God in his word says that he does this or that that their joy may be accomplished

---

6 Romans 5:5.

7 Compare 2 Corinthians 9:15; John 3:16.

8 Isaiah 54:8.

9 Romans 8:32; Matthew 26:28.

10 John 16:24.

and made full. Here my soul and all that was within me blessed God wonderfully for this sweetness of his love.[11]

On Tuesday morning my soul was more and more filled with that sweet sense of God's love in the death of Christ, and at the last was admirably comforted by finding God relieving me from my second burden…because God let me see that his apparent wrath in my wife's death was a real love to me. A greater mercy to me appeared therein than ever I saw before in anything that had befallen me, for thereby I saw God bringing me within the compass of the promises both of this life and of the life to come, which are contained in the gospel (2 Timothy 4:8). I saw God thereby recalling me from impenitence to repentance never to be repented of,[12] from security[13] unto wakefulness, from hardness of heart unto a melted and softed heart; in a word, from death of grace unto the life of grace.…Thereby I found God drawing me wonderfully more near and more familiarly unto him than ever before, and also coming, talking, dwelling with my soul more than ever before.[14] Is not this a sweet change, O my soul? and doth thou not bless God for it? Yes, O Lord, my soul and all that is within me blesseth thee for it.… Hereby God has prepared thee extraordinarily to glorify him, edify thy friends and comfort thyself with those true heavenly joys more than ever, either in life or death according to his good pleasure.

---

11 Compare Psalm 103:1.
12 2 Corinthians 7:9.
13 The meaning here is complacency, or a slothful self-reliance.
14 Compare Jeremiah 31:3; James 4:8; John 14:17–18; 2 Corinthians 6:16.

15

Continuing instant in prayer and meditation [1]

August 10, 14 & 15, 1633

On Friday morning I vowed unto the Lord that, if he would totally and finally deliver me from all my troubles, griefs, fears and perplexities, I should ever bless him for it, and in token of my thanksgiving turn all the Psalms into praises as I have turned them into prayers during my affliction. Thereafter I prayed unto the Lord humbly and earnestly because I was miserable, and he powerful to deliver; also confidently, my confidence being grounded upon God's threefold promise and my threefold experience. God's promise first by his prophet, Psalm 145:18, "The Lord is nigh unto all them that call upon him.... He will fulfil the desire of them that fear him; he also will hear their cry and will save them." The second promise being out of the mouth of Christ, who is Truth itself, Luke 11:9, "And I" (who cannot lie) "say unto you, 'Ask and it shall be given you, seek and ye shall find, knock and it shall be opened

---

1 *Diary, 1632–1639*, 104, 109, 111.

unto you. For everyone that asketh receiveth, and he that seeketh findeth, and to him that knocketh it shall be opened.'" The third promise is from the apostle [in] Philippians 4:6, "Be careful for nothing, but in everything by prayer and supplication with thanksgiving let your requests be made known unto God. And the peace of God which passeth all understanding shall keep your hearts and minds through Christ Jesus." My first experience of God's hearing my prayers and fulfilling his promises was in my sixteenth year, while I was a Latiner.[2] My second experience was immediately after my voyage into France, while I cried for protection to my voyage, and direction to my studies and a safe return. The third was immediately before my marriage, in his delivering me from temptations and blessing me so extraordinarily in my marriage.

On Tuesday morning…I was extraordinarily dejected with great heaviness and many tears. Thereafter…God moved me to mark the deceitfulness of man's heart in mourning, praying and praising, making us ever to look on sin as it relates to us…as it brings down upon the party God's wrath, both here and in hell's fire, while God directed me chiefly to mourn for sin as it was relative unto God by offending, grieving, angering of so loving a Father…and to pray for pardon of it rather as it grieved him than as it plagued me; and so rather in my repentance, prayer, praises to have an eye…unto God's glory than my own salvation…. Then God moved me, while I was in prayer, even to wish that, providing I blasphemed not God, to be tormented for ever in hell in case God would instead of me save a thousand souls which would not otherwise be saved, because I thought, "Lord I should prefer thy glory to my salvation, and a thousand in my stead would glorify thee far more than I, one person, could do." Then I was extraordinarily comforted by God promising that, seeing I had such an earnest desire of glorifying him…he would have a more special extraordinary care and tender-

---

2 Meaning "a Latin scholar."

ness to my salvation and consolation.

On Wednesday morning, meditating on Zachariah 12:10, I got my very heart poured out before God with abundance of tears when I looked on Christ's passion, his bloody sweat in the garden, and his crying on the cross, "My God, My God, why hast thou forsaken me?"[3]

Having mourned extraordinarily out of pity of Christ's death, and out of unspeakable grief that I should have been the cause of all, I abhorred my iniquities...more for the crucifying [of] Christ than for the bringing this cross upon me.... Then thereby I was extraordinarily comforted, being assured as it were, that seeing I pitied and mourned for Christ's sufferings...more than for myself, he...would the more pity and be compassionate unto my present miseries, chiefly when he saw me repeating his own prayer, "Abba Father, all things are possible unto thee: take away this cup (of affliction, temptation and confusion) from me; nevertheless not my will but thine be done."[4]

...From this meditation of Christ's passion I found sensibly (as daylight) my love inflamed, my faith strengthened, my hope confirmed, my repentance augmented and my desire and resolution to serve him...doubled, tripled, multiplied. Then heartily and confidently I prayed...for the augmentation of all those graces, for his direction to my confusion, his assistance against temptations and, in his own good time, for a deliverance from my present miseries.

---

3 Matthew 27:46.
4 Mark 14:36.

16

Choosing a calling [1]

August 1633

My good brother[2] fell to exhorting me to settle my resolutions concerning my calling, and by reasons persuaded me to continue in that which I had begun, letting me see my impatience for catechising on the one part, and a possibility to serve God and to do good in the advocateship. This his exhortation, Mr. Baillie's letters,[3] and the minister's direction in his sermon to use the ordinary means, all following one another in one morning, made me, out of reverence to God's providence therein, begin to resolve to settle myself therein....

On Monday...after praising and praying I resolved to keep my private fast unto God all this week for my deliverance from my troubles, fears and perplexities, for God's assisting me against temptation and directing me in my confusions chiefly concerning my

---

1 *Diary, 1632–1639*, 118, 126, 134–136.

2 His brother-in-law Robert Burnet (1592–1661), a lawyer who had married Johnston's sister Rachel.

3 Robert Baillie (1602–1662), a relative and minister, who had written encouraging Johnston to "follow out" his calling.

calling, wherein I pray the Lord…to direct me in the choosing… and to bless me in it…and to enable me in and by it to glorify him, edify his servants and my friends, and the poor people, and to work out my own salvation with fear and trembling[4]….

I fell to the reading of Perkins,[5] and finding my mind much settled thereby…I resolved to follow his rules…he directs us to examine unto what calling God does call us? 1. By our affection and inclination; 2. By our gifts.

Then I spent all the afternoon…to try by both whether I should apply myself to the ministry or the laws…I found indeed that I respected more and honoured in my mind the first more than the last, but that my affection and resolution carried me to the last, both because I saw my mind could not be ever bent on religious exercises, but fainted if it were not sometimes diverted to worldly occasions, as also because I durst not take the burden of more souls than mine own, of which alone I found every difficulty that I could work out its salvation…. So I found that ever my inclination was to serve God in this, fearing…lest sometime I should be diverted therefrom to another. And secondly, because I found my gifts not so fitted for the first as for the last, because my gift is rather dialectic than didactic, fitter for disputing pro and contra than for teaching solid grounds; then, because neither my invention, judgement nor memory was for handling of so deep mysteries, and that to the judgement of all…I have an evil scraped tongue, and so would have no utterance at all in preaching, for indeed I was never a good linguist either in Scots, French or Latin. But chiefly seeing the main point of that calling consists in catechising, whereof I am utterly incapable in respect of my natural hastiness, crossness and impatience…. As for the law, both my affection, my continual resolution

---

4 Philippians 2:12.

5 William Perkins, *A Treatise of the Vocations or Callings of Men (1603)*. William Perkins (1558–1602) was a theologian and key leader of the Puritan movement in the Church of England.

since my childhood, my plying of my studies to that end, the manifold occasions of furthering me in it, my gifts being disputative, naturally fitted for it, and chiefly the warrant of the apostle commanding me to remain in the calling wherein I was called (1 Corinthians 7:20)…much settled my mind and made me resolve that, having craved God's direction instantly in my choice, and then his blessing on my choice, to fall to my book next week.

That resolution…was much furthered by reading Genesis 3:19… also Matthew 25 about the servants that received the talents… Colossians 3:22…2 Thessalonians 3:10…. My mind being much moved by these passages to be settled in a calling, and then being confirmed in my first resolution by Perkin's rules, but chiefly by that 1 Corinthians 7:20, I blessed God most heartily for the settling of my mind so well.

17

Charity, humility and comfort [1]

August 25-26, 1633

After [the] sermon the first thought that came in my mind was that
God who was so gracious in comforting me under my trouble
would be as gracious by delivering me in his own time from it;[2]
also he that gave me the heart to relieve the distressed even above
my power, would, for that end, augment my power.[3] Then I sent to
the poor in the Tolbooth[4] three dollars out of obedience to God's
joining ever together the giving of alms unto fasting and prayer.
Then…my heart melted like water in an extraordinary manner,
seeing nothing in me to discontinue God's wrath or move his love,
but on the contrary things, even in my best actions…deserving, yea
drawing down God's wrath on me and withholding his love…..
Whereat being wonderfully humbled unto the very hells, and going
desperately out of myself unto Christ, I was on a sudden comforted

---

1 *Diary, 1632–1639*, 146–147.
2 Compare 2 Corinthians 1:4,10.
3 Compare 2 Corinthians 8:3.
4 Edinburgh's notorious prison.

by that of Malachi 3:6, "I am the Lord, I change not, therefore ye sons of Jacob are not consumed," and by recalling God's bygone calling me when I was in the very mouth of hell, deserving the deepest pit thereof. What said I to my soul? Despair not at the sight of thy abominable corruption which thou thinkest will continue his wrath.... Dost thou not remember how God in his free love to thee through Christ did pass over all thy transgressions at thy calling; and while thou didst most deserve hell…then he raised thee, being dead in sins and trespasses (Romans 5; Ephesians 2), even not only against thy deserts but contrary to thy desires, which were only bent on hellish conceits, and gave the right unto the kingdom of heaven? Will he, being unchangeable in himself and in his gifts (Romans 11:29), not far rather now pass by the transgressions of his child…? Be therefore of good comfort, for as the Lord lives who was found of thee when thou sought him not,[5] he will find thee in far more mercy when thou so earnestly seekest it of him.[6]

On Monday afternoon, while I was writing this, my mind was extraordinarily illuminated and comforted by the sight of God's free, undeserved, yea undesired love in my calling from hell to heaven, from sin to repentance. Then God moved me extraordinarily by this meditation that affliction was the trial of affection… now it was the day of my trying the constancy of his friendship. Then with floods of tears and inexpressible groans repeated I unto God all my petitions, ever mourning especially and craving pardon for the imperfections of my fasting, confessing, praying, praising.

---

5 Compare Isaiah 65:1.

6 See Proverbs 8:17.

18

Retrospection and rejoicing [1]

November 26, 1633

I read over my marks[2] of Hosea and Joel, adhering chiefly to Hosea 2, 6 and 14 and to Joel 2:12, which ever bred to me much comfort. After that the Lord opened my eyes to see his wonderful goodness to me during all the time of my trouble, whereat he made my heart to leap within me for joy, and my mouth to cry that he had never dealt so bountifully and compassionately with any creature as he had dealt with me, suppose never one had so grieved and offended him as I had done. He let me see that all his works with me in my trouble were as many wonders and miracles, both in respect of his power and love, whereby he made me to swear that God's mercy was above all his works, that he pitied his saints as a tender-hearted father pities his children, that all his promises were full of truth, all his works full of love, all his footsteps continually dropped fatness to his own.[3]

---

1 *Diary, 1632–1639*, 172.
2 i.e. marked passages.
3 Psalm 103:11,13; 65:11.

He let me see that he had heard two of my petitions and fulfilled two of his promises by forcing me to acknowledge...that the day of my trouble, which seemed to proceed from his wrath and tend to my wreck, proceeded from his love and tended to my weal[4]... that he had been with me in my trouble, directing me in my confusions, comforting me in my afflictions and upholding me in my temptations. Hereby my soul, astonished at his goodness, was forced to bless him, vowed to serve him, to rely on him in all my troubles and especially in this present, even that he would perfect the work which he had begun[5]...hear my third prayer and perform his third promise concerning my delivery out of it.

---

4 Meaning "welfare."
5 Philippians 1:6.

19

Reflections following the rejection of a new marriage proposal[1]

November 30 - December 1, 1633

"O Lord, thou knowest to what an ebb all my hopes was brought low, and how every thought, every wish in my mind contradicted one another, how the fear of folks…railing and jesting at my sudden change and volatility dissuaded me; how on the other hand the desire to be freed of my temptations persuaded me [to seek remarriage]…. Betwixt these two, as the Israelites betwixt Megiddo and the Red Sea[2]…I stood amazed and astonished at my own confusion, crying with Jehoshaphat, 'Lord I know not what to do, nor what to think, nor what to wish…but my eyes are on thee.'[3] O Lord, cast me in all sickness, griefs, torments of mind and body before thou leave me in this strait…or permit me to dishonour thee, scandalize my profession, offend my friends and aggravate my own condemnation; but thou that delivered, settled, blessed me before, deliver,

---

1   *Diary, 1632–1639*, 179–180.
2   Exodus 14:2.
3   2 Chronicles 20:12.

settle and bless me now for Christ's sake."

... At evening, in my confusion, I began to cry for God's direction, but, woe is me, for here I saw my natural frailty, that where I was most...resolved to be instant with God, in this particular I was most lukewarm and my prayers were slept over for that night. God be merciful to me for it and thereby make me know more and more how all our earnest desires, settled resolutions and urgent necessities with oppressing troubles, are not able to excite our drowsy spirits unto prayer except God's Spirit of prayer be poured out on us. After supper, my confused contradictory thoughts and desires oppressed me so heavily as they rendered me stupid, senseless, yea almost hopeless and faithless. Having reflected on this state I shouted, "Lord save me, for my faith perishes,"[4] and with many tears I cried for the continuance of my faith, which I had sometimes well builded on good grounds, but now found it shaken by contrariety of appearances, whereby I saw and learned that it was the hardest task in the world to believe God on his bare word when outward means, tending to what we aimed at, failed us and contrary appearances do beset us round about. In this heavy plight, I was upheld by remembering Abraham's faith (Romans 4; Hebrews 11), which I prayed God, first, to make me imitate and, second, to have the like issue.

Having considered my present estate, I was filled with gall and bitterness, oppressed with groans and tears twice...I saw nothing... but signs of a heavy wrath and tokens of a great destruction. I pray... that my greatest enemy never see that sight or feel so doleful a mourning as I did. Nevertheless, I groaned, roared, wrestled as I could, resolving for my confusions to do nothing hastily and rather to suffer private trouble than give public scandal. In the Kirk...we read Acts 10 where God tells Cornelius he had heard his prayers and did send Peter to him...and we sang Psalm 38:16 and...Psalm 39, most

---

4   Matthew 14:30.

fit for my present estate.... [In the] afternoon, I considered how some of my hopes now had failed me, and so how difficult a thing it is to discern betwixt the suggestions of our spirits and the motions of God's Spirit. By this event, may I learn this lesson: never to limit the Holy One of Israel again,[5] for the very prefixing to God a set time of delivering us is the high way to make him prolong the day of our distress, and the prescribing to God the object, the manner and the particular means of my deliverance is the direct course to hinder the Lord, if not from delivering at all, yet from delivering by that means.... Whereas the submitting thy will to his, both concerning the time and the means, is the fittest way to move him to a gracious and speedy deliverance.

---

5 Psalm 78:41.

20

A new year's meditation [1]

January 1, 1634

On…the first day of the new year, I meditated first on all God's blessings bestowed on me all the last year…for which with great floods of tears I blessed God most heartily, and subscribed to that maxim, "That God had never been so good to any creature as to me." Secondly, I passed over all my sins and offences…confessing them unto God by order of time, whereupon I subscribed the other maxim, "That never soul had been so wicked, false, perjured, ungrateful and abominable to God as I had been." Thirdly, I prayed the Lord most instantly to accept my praises and to discharge all bygones, so in time to come and particularly in this year, 1634, to rule, govern, direct, provide, deliver and bless me, so as to keep me from all that will dishonour him, scandalize my profession, offend my friends and aggravate my condemnation. But on the other part, for Christ Jesus' sake, that he would honour himself, edify his servants, content my friends, work out my salvation in all my

---

1 *Diary, 1632–1639*, 189–190.

courses, both of my calling and my private settling, and particularly he would direct me in this business[2] I have now in hand.

I pray God the first meditation may, as it should, strengthen my faith; the second may augment my repentance; the third may stir up the spirit of...supplication, which three I would receive from God as the best new year's gift in the world.

---

2 Johnston was now courting Helen Hay.

21

Reliance on God [1]

March 10, 1634

On Monday morning, my heart being ravished with an assurance of my remission, I know not with what unspeakable filial confidence and conjuring earnestness I put up all my petitions to God, especially with greatest liberty and abundance of tears that concerning my marriage,[2] renouncing first my own affections for it, or my friends against it; mistrusting both…and resigning both in God's hands so that I would neither pray for it nor against it. So despairing of any good to follow upon mine or their desires, and running as it were out of myself and from them, I took my burden and cast it on God,[3] telling him I trusted, I relied only on his love and not on theirs nor my own, on his wisdom…his power and not on theirs or mine…with many strong cries, groans and tears that he would neither fulfil my will nor theirs but only accomplish that

---

1 *Diary, 1632–1639*, 202–203.

2 To Helen Hay: though she returned his affection, Johnston faced opposition from friends and relatives.

3 Compare Psalm 55:22.

which tended most to his glory, the weal[4] of his servants and our salvation.... After this my mistrust of myself and trust in God, with extraordinary instancy I urged him to accept this charge, and with argumenting confidence mingled with tears I conjured him to manifest all his divine attributes both of indulgence and providence to me in hindering or furthering of it, because he had ever hitherto done so to me especially in the first, because he had under my trouble given me a heart to pray for it, had promised to hear me, had made me conceive hope in his goodness for it by reason of both....

At night in my own chamber God dealt wonderfully with me.... The assurance of my remission now sealed up to my soul, my despair of myself and reliance on him, my filial unutterable confidence of my Father's love, power and wisdom made me with groans, sighs, cries unspeakable to reiterate all my morning's petitions to God as my Father, to Christ as to my Saviour, to the Spirit as to my Comforter, for which liberty and communion...my soul and body blessed God heartily.

---

4 Meaning "welfare."

22

Spiritual warfare [1]

May 22 & 29, 1634

On Thursday…my eyes were opened to see that all my life hitherto was nothing but a continual fight betwixt the Trinity on the one part to save me, and the devil with myself to damn me. When my thoughts reflected on both God's ways and my own hitherto, I saw as clearly as the sun at noonday a most continual strife for my soul betwixt those two, as betwixt Michael and the devil for Moses' body. [2]

I saw the Lord turning all my own ways, his ways, the devil's ways, the world's ways with me…of my youth, my marriage, my widow-hood, to my weal [3] and salvation. I saw on the contrary the devil and my corruption perverting all, defiling all, striving to turn all… to my eternal ruin, by making me unthankful, forgetful, [an] abuser of his blessings whereby God strove to allure me, impatient, mur-muring, passionate, distrustful…. Upon sight of this combat, my soul prayed, contrary to myself (my corruption which is the most

---

1 *Diary, 1632–1639*, 213–214; 222–223.
2 Jude 9.
3 Meaning "welfare."

part of myself, Goliath like in respect of the little David of grace) that the Lord might overcome, that Satan and myself might be overthrown. Hereupon my soul also was amazed at God's wonderful mercy to take such pains to save them who fought against him to be damned. Thereafter in meditation, the Lord humbled me more at the sight of my sins by consideration of God's mercies bestowed on me in the meantime of my sinning, and made me more sensible of God's mercies by consideration of my sins which I was committing against him during the receipt of those mercies....Thereafter, in my resignation and recommendation, I was much moved, and I got abundance of tears, blessed be the Lord for this liberty....

After my particular passing over all God's ways for me, and mine contrary to him and his at my petitions, the devil cast ever in my teeth, as sufficient cause of their denial, the sins of my adversity, widowhood, wooing. Whereupon my soul retorted,

1. That the Lord passed ever by my deserts and answered my desires, as appeared particularly in all my life hitherto.
2. That those [sins] now could neither withhold good or draw down evil on me, because their pardon was subscribed by Christ's blood and sealed to my conscience both inwardly and outwardly in the last communion.

Whereupon my soul, by a divine excellence out of myself as it were lifting up my tearful eyes and grieved yet confident heart to Christ Jesus, I challenged him of his promise, and said, "Even between thee Christ Jesus and thy Father be it, if now I be scourged for that for which thou hast satisfied. Show then thy satisfaction applied to me before thy Father, and tell him he cannot twice take payment for one debt;[4] manifest now to me the power of thy intercession with him; remember thou interceded for the first, remember

---

4 See Romans 8:1.

thou let me…see thee interceding in the Scheins yard for me under my trouble. Thy credit is now engaged, let me know that thy Father denies thee nothing" (John 11:42).

Whereupon I thought I saw the Son of God putting up all these and many more…before his Father. My soul at this time was almost out of itself; blessed be the Lord God for this favour also, for who has such an intercessor cannot but come good speed.

23

Acknowledging God's mercies: engagement to Helen Hay [1]

August 14, 1634

At evening, before supper, we prayed; but after supper, while I was sleeping on her knee, the Lord in an instant so wakened me with a most sensible sight of God's inexpressible kindness to us in this particular (wherein our hearts were forced to acknowledge that, in all the world, we could never have made a fitter choice) so that, falling down on our knees with tears in our eyes and melting hearts we acknowledged most sensibly God's fatherly love, mercy, providence, indulgence to us in it. We prayed earnestly that this sight of his pardoning, sparing, comforting, directing, delivering mercies contrary to our deserts and beyond our expectation, disappointing our fears, hearing our prayers, answering to our wishes, fulfilling our hopes, performing his promises, might inflame our souls with love towards so loving a Father, might renew our godly sorrow for offending…might increase our faith in the assurance of our eternal

---

1 *Diary, 1632–1639*, 241–242.

salvation as also of our temporal deliveries out of our subsequent troubles; might augment our patience under God's hands in new straits; might stir us up unto a sensible thankfulness for so sensible favours, and at the last might arm us against the temptations of our subsequent estate, and quicken us to obey and serve hereafter so loving a Father, so gracious a Sovereign, so merciful a Master. From the bottom of our hearts we prayed thus to the Lord, ever blessing for his great undeserved blessings, especially for his love clear shining to us in them.

24

Usefulness of recorded memories: in prosperity [1]

February 7, 1637

The Lord brought back to my mind out of what I had been reading in my papers two things: first, his moving me so earnestly…to pray for death if the Lord had nothing to do with me in my life for his glory or his servants' weal, [2] which gave me some hope the Lord yet had ado with me, albeit I cannot see wherein. Second, his manner of dealing with me…on the Saturday of the approving my first marriage, renewed to me on Saturday, July 27 in the Scheins alley under my calamity, with the Spirit's immediate prayer annexed thereto. These both bred in me a hope yet to see the visibility of my delivery therein prayed for and promised, as also a resolution to follow the same solid course for getting a blessing to my calling, to wit, first by taking away sin by repentance, which is the cause of all evil and crosses…and, on the other part, by endeavouring for, and

---

1 *Diary, 1632–1639*, 247.

2 Meaning "welfare."

entertaining of, a soft, tender, poured-out heart to draw down his spiritual and temporal blessings upon me. To the obtaining of both, the Lord grant and bless my resolution and endeavour.

25

Union and communion with God [1]

April 23, 1637

On Sunday…in my own chamber it pleased the Lord to communicate himself fully to my soul…. Between three and six at night, while I was walking alone and meditating on the nature, essence, names, attributes, words, works of a Deity, my whole body took a shuddering and extreme coldness seized on all my joints, especially on the roots of my hair which stood all stiff, bent up from the crown of my head; my eyes stood wide open, never closing albeit rivers of tears ran down my cheeks; my tongue struck dumb; my hands at will now reached out as it were to receive a Deity, now clasped in…. This was the temper of my body, while…my soul was transported out of myself and fixed upon…an incomprehensible Deity, like lightnings glancing in at a window: first, his nature in general, then the unity in trinity, trinity in unity, then his attributes of justice, mercy, power, presence, wisdom, truth, then his works all in order first of creation, then of election, redemption, justification, sancti-

---

1   *Diary, 1632–1639*, 251–253.

fication, eternal glorification…then the application of all to my own soul….At the glance of every one after another the shuddering wakened, my hair bended and a new rush of tears gushed out… my soul was crying without utterance, "Deity, Deity, I adore, I adore, I adore." While my soul ran sometimes upon the contemplation of a Deity, my thoughts were in a confusion and some sort of fear; but when it ran upon the conception of the Trinity and especially of the second person as clothed with our human nature, my sight was more clear and sense more sweet. Then my soul, as it were, separated from my body and so united as to be made one with him.

In the twinkling of an eye…behold the catalogue of all my sins done either before or since my calling, presented to my memory… whereat I began to tremble, my soul ever crying without utterance, "God's mercy"…. On a sudden, while I am thus praying, behold a new reel of all God's favours…on soul, body or affairs old or recent, whereat my soul revived crying, "Hallelujah…Father glorify thyself in my life and death…grant thou mercy to my misery and grace to my gracelessness…give thyself to me and take myself to thee that thou may be mine and I may be thine." I thought…that my Jesus took my heart in his hand and knit it and wrapped it within the heart of God, so that I found God as it were within my heart possessing and filling all the corners and holes thereof, and I found my heart and soul within the heart of God contemplating, adoring, embracing his…inward parts. I could not then conceive, far less now express, how persuading and persuaded I was by present reflecting thoughts on my present contemplation that God was mine, yea fully mine, and I was his, yea totally his, that he was mine with all his blessings and followers, and I was his with all my infirmities and burdens. All the night thereafter, yea even this morning while I am writing this down, the stamp of yesternight's impressions cleaves fast to my soul, and my thoughts, desires…are as unsatiable, as unexpressable. The Lord God open my eyes by a second sight to see his favour, aim and end, with my use of this odd sea of transporting motions, whereby in so inexpressible a bountiful manner and measure he communicates himself to…sinful dust and ashes,[2] and makes me…to acknowledge his Son's promise to have been heard…that I have been made one with him and he one with me.[3]

The Lord makes me to apprehend that this clear day will have a dark night, and this fair calm will have a foul storm. The Lord give me the right use of this and prepare me for that, and let this stand for a testimony against myself of consolation in new weakenings of mind, and of conviction on my yielding to subsequent temptations.

---

2 Compare Genesis 18:27.
3 Compare John 17:21; 14:20.

26

Seeking divine blessing for work [1]

May 1637

I got motion in praying to God for his blessing on my calling, because I was pushed forward and shut forth by himself after many doubts and perplexities, and because I relied neither upon friends without, nor gifts within, but only trusting his providence, assistance, indulgence. I went to that calling in the name, in the strength and arm of the Most High; not as Goliath, trusting in my own natural gifts, but as David, relying on my God, the God of Israel[2]…. The Lord brought to my mind how many, especially young men… depended much on those two props of their own natural qualifications of judgement, wit, learning, utterance…and outward occasions of friends, employments or means, which both might fail, and the Lord in his justice might either curb or curse both. Despairing of both, rejecting both, I cast my calling on God alone, who not only in the ministerial (in which most ordinarily) but even in other

---

1 *Diary, 1632–1639*, 265–267.
2 1 Samuel 17:45.

callings, can both remove natural gifts from those that have them and give them to them that wants them, and also will sometimes more bless and assist the lesser and leave the greater....

On Sunday...to hold my affections waking, I thought it good... to seek God himself, and...his blessing on my calling. Whereupon the Lord brought to my mind some Scripture, especially the Lord's calling Moses (Exodus 3) and his answer: Exodus 4:10, "O my Lord, I am not eloquent, neither heretofore, nor since thou hast spoken to thy servant: but I am slow of speech and of a slow tongue." And the Lord said unto him, "Who hath made man's mouth? or who maketh the dumb or deaf or the seeing or the blind? have not I the Lord? Now therefore go, and I will be with thy mouth and teach thee what thou shalt say" [verses 11–12].... The application in every particular was borne in upon me. First, that the Lord had called me to that calling and after many doubts entered me, and then my back-falling because I neither had knowledge, nor wit, nor judgement, invention, nor memory, nor utterance, nor experience, nor employment, neither before God's calling nor from the time God had spoken to me.... Then the Lord's reply by reentering me this winter anew again, by reviving my hopes, assisting me in the occasions which his providence sent me and casting me in employments. Then my heart cried to the Lord that, of dumb he would make me speak the terms of my calling; of deaf, to hear, conceive and understand; of blind and ignorant, to see...through the doubts and difficulties thereof; that he would say to me, "Go on in thy calling, I will be with thee, thy mind, thy invention, thy judgement, thy memory, thy mouth; I will teach thee what to conceive, invent, remember, judge or say." Lord, hear; Lord grant; Lord fulfil. In like manner, the application of all the passages in Exodus 31 anent[3] Bezaleel and Aholiab unto me in my calling was borne in upon me; likewise that in Jeremiah 1:4.... All this was applied to me from within, notwithstanding some scruple I had that it could not be extended to any other than the ministerial calling.

---

3 An archaic Scottish word meaning "about" or "concerning."

27

Anxiety over the church's welfare [1]

July & August 1637

Upon Sunday, July 23, that black, doleful Sunday to the Kirk and Kingdom of Scotland, the service book began to be read in the Kirks of Edinburgh.[2] At the beginning thereof there rose such a tumult, such an outcrying...as the like was never seen...I pray the Lord to make his own children with tears and cries to pray against this spiritual plague of Egyptian darkness covering the light of the gospel shining in this nation....The Lord in public assisted me to recommend it to the Lord in my family with fervency, while I was in private having...a little grudge in my mind at the Lord's providence in not occasionating a vent to those thoughts he had furnished me with in that particular to which he had called me[3]....

---

1   *Diary, 1632–1639*, 265–267.

2   The ritualistic liturgy produced by Charles I and Archbishop Laud, in consultation with the Scottish bishops, and imposed on the Kirk (The Church of Scotland) by royal proclamation.

3   i.e. the law.

The Lord brought to mind and pressingly applied to my soul what he had said to Jonah about the gourd[4]..."Did I not call thee to this calling? Any gift thou hast for the general, is it not from me? Did thou not despair and have not I made thee to hope? Found thou not as it were in thyself an impossibility...of any ability in this calling, and now thou findest my immediate assistance enabling thee? Any thought, meditation, study in this particular came it not from me? May I not retire it when I will? and as by my presence thou findest thy spirit edged, thy mind cleared, thy memory firmed, so by my absence art thou not presently dull, dead, dumb? Should thou not thank me cheerfully for what benefit, credit, name, hope thou hast rather than to grudge at this little restraint?"...Whereupon my mind being settled confessed my rashness, craved pardon, prayed for his assistance.

Upon Sunday morning, August 6, in private first and then in my family publicly, I recommended, with great fervency and abundance of tears, the church of Scotland unto the Lord, as tending more to God's glory than my salvation, as the ruin thereof were more dishonourable to God than my destruction.... It came in my mind that, if we licked up this vomit of Romish superstition again, the Lord in his wrath would vomit us out, and was not, like man, to return to his vomit again.[5] The Lord engraved in my mind that of the prophet, "There is poison in the pot."[6]

---

4 Jonah 4:10.
5 Compare 2 Peter 2:22; Revelation 3:16.
6 2 Kings 4:40.

28

Consolation amidst confusion[1]

October 29, 1637

On Sunday… I got some good both in the morning and evening recommending all over to God. After I had read the covenant contained in Deuteronomy 29 and 30, I prayed the Lord to direct my particular carriage in all these affairs. I found all as it were wrong, the disposition of my mind, body, estate, name, calling, all going down the wind, which made me call God's mercy and deprecate his justice. I remembered that many times the Lord had given me many fair, even outward, glances and hopes, and then had removed them, but after the removal of the first had sent me the second… so that now it might be the Lord, having fairly entered me in my calling, might now interrupt my hopes and split them asunder….

I enquired about my going to Linlithgow[2] and following the session as David about Ziklag,[3] whether I should follow them. I

---

1 *Diary, 1632–1639*, 271–272.

2 The legal term had been transferred from Edinburgh to Linlithgow, as a result of the gathering crisis, which had a disastrous impact on Johnston's law practice.

3 1 Samuel 30.

prayed the Lord to let me find the more particularly his providence, the more need I stood of it in the midst of so great confusions. I thought seriously with myself that Christianity was a great blessing, for a Christian has always a strong tower of refuge to hide himself in the day of evil under the wings of the Lord's merciful providence,[4] and has ever a back door of prayer open in the midst of all confusions. I thought seriously that God's eternal love in Christ was a sure rock, foundations of all our lawful hopes and desires in the day of trouble,[5] while all other worldly retreats and refuges are but Egyptian reeds, sandy foundations and vanity of vanities, yea vexation of spirit.[6]

I prayed the Lord that I might find the constant course of his former favourable providence continued with me and on all I put my hands to, that I might have hereafter great reason...to praise the Lord and set his work down here.[7]

---

4 Compare Proverbs 18:10; Psalm 61:3; 17:8.
5 Compare Psalm 27:5; Isaiah 28:16.
6 2 Kings 18:21; Matthew 7:26–27; Ecclesiastes 1:2,14.
7 i.e. in his diary.

29

Answering the call to public service [1]

November 20 - December 5, 1637

Mr. David Dick[2] told me that my Lord Laudin[3] and he had been resolving to lay the charge of pleading upon me if either the noblemen or the town of Edinburgh were troubled.[4]

I answered [that] the Lord knew my insufficiency, but if the Lord gave me a lawful calling, both inwardly and outwardly, I durst not doubt of his assistance, whereof I had so manifest proofs in business [which] concerned not his glory so much, so that I would neither refuse the calling nor distrust the assistance.... Thinking upon this in the morning, I was glad but to have one thought that who knows but this was the occasion whereunto all God's extraordinary dealings has had some relation to in preparing me to it, and but to have

---

1 *Diary, 1632–1639*, 273, 275–278, 280–281.

2 David Dickson (*c.*1583–1663) was the minister of the parish of Irvine.

3 John Campbell, Earl of Loudoun (1598–1662), who became prominent among the Covenanting nobles of Scotland.

4 By legal action for resisting the service book.

some hope of a liberty once to declare the Lord's goodness and to maintain his worship, to be but a mean instrument thereof. My heart conceived it as a great happiness…to think there was a possibility of the Lord's mind to glorify himself in some measure…by my calling, endeavours and experience….

Upon Friday morning, the Lord having brought to mind for to cast in a mite of my weak endeavours in my calling to the rebuilding God's house, and casting down the Kingdom of Antichrist, by collecting together a note of the most remarkable acts of Parliament…, I prayed the Lord to pour upon me the spirit of my calling in this particular act thereof so immediately tending to his glory; so to sanctify my memory, judgement and wit as to gather therefrom the powerfullest, cleanest consequences, which may further the work in hand…. Conform to my petition, I found the Lord's assistance that day, and on Saturday morning after I had meditated on Psalm 127. But on Sunday, I was dead all day…I suspect among others this was a chief cause of my deadness, that on this day, being a private fast and so devoted to practical devotion…my mind was taken up with the controversies of the time…. But upon Monday morning, being to study the point of the King's prerogative…I began by God's direction to meditate on Psalm 143, and while I was meditating on the eighth verse, "Cause me to hear thy lovingkindness in the morning, for I trust in thee; cause me to know the way wherein I should walk, for I lift up my soul unto thee," my affection was moved in the application thereof, and brought to my mind the application of all the former verses. Then the tears trickled down my cheeks and my soul, finding the Lord's immediate presence, reminded him of his former particular unspeakable favours…and begged the continuance of both…. Then my soul took greater boldness to crave knowledge of the way wherein she should walk in these difficult, defective times; and as Samuel said, so did my soul,

"Speak Lord, for thy servant heareth;[5] direct thou and thy servant shall follow." Then the Lord, as it were, asked, "What if I put thee upon this difficult piece of service now in hand?" My soul answered, "Lord, thou knowest the stammering...of my tongue, the weakness of my wit, the unclear, unsolid indistinctness of my judgement, the slippery slidiness of my memory. What shall I say, O Lord? Thou knowest thy servant ten thousand times better than he does himself, how ungifted, unfit, unready...."

Upon Tuesday, my soul beginning to speak with God was transported in a fervent desire for mercy to my personal sins and the iniquities of all my faculties and members, of wit, memory, judgement, tongue, hand, for washing, cleansing, rinsing of them through and through, lest my sins of them, as weapons of unrighteousness, should withhold the Lord from calling or employing them to be instruments of his glory. Thus with great abundance of tears and I know not what inexpressible...desires, with a reflecting thought that the Lord hereby was preparing me for I know not what public glorifying him...my prayer...with a sudden ejaculation of a confident hope [was], "Lord, call, I shall obey; bid go and I shall go." O for a calling, an occasion, an immediate influence and assistance. O I durst not doubt of the last getting the first, because the Lord would prepare me for the work and it for me. What hinders this influence but sin? What stops, interrupts, eclipses the union and communion of the soul with God...but sin? What dims that nature's and reason's light once given to Adam but sin? ... Being pardoned and grace granted, with a calling inviting, I durst not doubt of the communication of light and grace from him, of restoring, for that time in that act, nature's and reason's strength for to agent his own business according to his promise, to his glory...

[On nomination as the nobles' advocate] I told my lord [Loudon] at length of my trouble about my irresolution to a calling, my fear

---

5 1 Samuel 3:10.

to be distracted in private retirings, my desire to be exercised in some occasion immediately tending to God's glory, then of my resolution at last of my lesson…I told him I was so far from being afraid by any worldly fear, that I thought the charge such a happiness as for the discharging of it answerably to the charge I could be content with God's will to dissolve me thereafter…. On the other part, I was noways induced by any worldly aims or respects, wherewith in this cause I would not corrupt the spirituality of my desires and designs…but that the Lord should be my only client and rewarder as I wished he might be my assister…. After dinner, my ordinary[6] being Romans 9 (with David's answer to Araunah, 2 Samuel 24:24, "Neither will I offer burnt offerings to the Lord of that which cost me nothing" and shall I gain worldly of my spiritual duty, to the which I am as much bound by my oath in the confession of my faith as any word given me? … I have been ever well paid by my God, both outwardly and inwardly…) confirmed me in my resolution to meddle with no man's monies as my client in this business, but only with my Lord and Saviour.

---

6 i.e. Johnston's regular Bible reading.

30

Godly household government[1]

January 6, 1638

Upon Friday, Lisbie, James' mammie,[2] having committed theft and drunkenness...instead of confessing her fault covered it with denials...whereat my wife being irritated put her to the gate. On Saturday night I was urged to receive her home again upon her repentance and promise of amendment. I called her before the whole family and showed her the great guiltiness of her fourfold fault, theft, drunkenness, lying and swearing, with all the aggravating circumstances and the judgements of God hanging over her head, which I was forced to denounce against her in the name of the eternal God, that if she made not use of this warning by repentance and amendment, that the visible judgements of God should follow her not only eternally in hell, but even in this life...and that this present warning would either prove sensibly a warning of mercy to her if she repented and kept her vow, or of justice to be the

---

1   *Diary, 1632–1639*, 293–294.
2   The wet-nurse of his son James.

savour of death unto death if she did not. Hereupon, after a long, sensible reproof and exhortation expressed out of my mouth by a present felt assistance and guidance of God's Spirit, I was moved in the immediate subsequent prayer to recommend my whole family to God with great earnestness, to confess their sins to God, with great motion to deprecate the Lord's wrath and judgement, which we daily provoke, to beg his mercy and grace in Christ and the happy event of that night's warning in mercy to all the family, and to resolve and command all the family for this end to keep the morrow, being the Lord's Sabbath, as a particular fast…for a particular confession of sin, supplication for mercy and grace, thanksgiving for the Lord's favour. It pleased the Lord by some of my words in the prayer mightily to waken Anna's[3] mind, reminding her of some of her vows…and her backsliding from them.

---

3 Anna Rae, Johnston's widowed sister-in-law.

31

Reflecting on unmerited mercies past and present[1]

January 17, 1638

Upon Wednesday morning…I arose about half five hours,[2] and… spent two hours in praising and praying, for the Lord brought so suddenly to my mind an epitome of all his former dealings with me….The Lord forced me to acknowledge…that he had heard my petitions, granted my prayers, fulfilled my hopes, satisfied my very wishes and prevented my fears, performed his promises related in this diarium[3] by…his employing, exercising and wonderfully assisting…his unworthy, unable servant in this main business concerning his glory…. But when I came to this last of the Lord's deigning to bid me go speak, study, write, plead for himself, his church, his worship—the honourablest, the happiest (albeit the heaviest) charge ever committed to creature—my heart did burst, neither being able to contain nor express the greatness of God's goodness in the calling,

---

1 *Diary, 1632–1639*, 297–300.
2 i.e. 4:30 a.m.
3 Meaning "diary."

or of my happiness in the being called and guided in this work of God, wherein to be employed and thereby to glorify my glorious God, I thought it did far exceed the very happiness of being glorified in heaven. Thus, not knowing what to speak or what to think, my heart without expression acknowledged my cup to run over; my lot to have fallen in pleasant places, and all the Lord's footsteps to drop fatness and marrow in my lap.[4] I exclaimed without voice in the thought of Mephibosheth's expression,[5] "What is thy servant, that thou shouldest look upon such a dead, dumb, deaf dog as I am?' ... Among men, what am I? The vilest, filthiest, crookedest, senselessest of mankind. Who has so often disobeyed thy precepts, misbelieved thy promises, slighted thy threats as I? Who so oft has hardened their own heart, blindfolded their mind, cauterised wittingly…their conscience as I? Who so oft has broken his vows… as I?… Who so oft wallowed himself in idolatry, will worship, blasphemy, breach of the Sabbath, disobedience, wronging their neighbour in life, goods, chastity, name and by concupiscence as I in the sight of God and my own conscience? But above all, …who has so oft forsaken the presence of God, a felt, found, experimented fountain of living waters of consolation, direction, salvation, of grace, of glory, and digged to themselves rotten cisterns of pleasures, profits, preferments, which in their own knowledge…can hold no water at all but of vanity and vexation, as I, I, I, miserable I, guilty above all expression or conception of this crimson sin of double dye?[6] And yet thou, great God of Israel, art my God from my mother's belly[7]…thou art acquainted with all my ways[8] and so directs and cares for me in them all as if thy eye looked to none… thy heart loved none other but this miserable wretch with whom

---

4 Psalm 23:5; 16:6; 65:11; 63:5.
5 2 Samuel 9:8.
6 Compare Jeremiah 2:13; Ecclesiastes 2:11; Isaiah 1:18.
7 Psalm 22:10.
8 Psalm 139:3.

thou delightest to talk and walk in so particular a manner....Thou makest me remember the kindness of my youth, the love of thy espousals, when I went after thee in the wilderness[9] and entered on the valley of Achor, the door of hope.[10]...But since now thou deignest to pick out thy unworthy...servant as one amongst a thousand... what can thy servant say but acknowledge the truth of thy promise (Micah 7:15)...(Ezekiel 36:11)...exclaim in obedience of thy precept, 'Wilt thou not from this time cry unto me, My father, thou art the guide of my youth?' (Jeremiah 3:4). O my Father, thou wert and art the guide of my youth, and surely goodness and mercy shall follow me all the days of my life, and I will dwell in the house of the Lord forever."[11]

---

9 Jeremiah 2:2.
10 Hosea 2:15.
11 Psalm 23:6.

32

Counting the cost [1]

January 22, 1638

Upon Monday morning…after reading over and meditating upon Psalm 43, my mind running upon…Mr. Robert Burnet's[2] warnings that this business would not only crush all my hopes of profit, credit, ease, respect, payment of debt, provision for my children by my calling, but also endanger my present estate, calling, means, yea my life and person, I began to desire my own soul to think seriously, constantly, resolutely upon these things. That we should not enter the spiritual warfare of Christianity without resolution to deny ourselves,[3] our hopes, desires, designs, profit, pleasure, etc.; but far less should I enter this special barras[4] of a particular combat for maintenance of the truth and opposition to idolatry against authority, power, might and wisdom, without an absolute, free, unreserved, undaunted resolution to take my life and all in my hand, to lay them

---

1 *Diary, 1632–1639*, 306–307.
2 Johnston's brother-in-law.
3 Compare Matthew 16:24.
4 An archaic word meaning "an arena for public combat."

down at the feet of God, and under him of man, for the cause in hand, and so…not only to be an actor…in this business for others, but to be a patient, a sufferer myself. These thoughts, I cannot deny, jumbled and troubled nature in me, but made the grace of God in me to acknowledge that it were the honourablest case, condition and charge that ever I could be in, to wish that the Lord would even honour his unworthy servant with the crown of martyrdom; to pray earnestly that the Lord would settle my resolution, prepare my soul and body beforehand for the trial, uphold…and direct me under it, and in his own time deliver me out of it, either by an outward delivery (if it be his will) or rather by an inward constancy and patience, going through and through it to the grave.

33

Christian foreknowledge[1]

February 11-12, 1638

On Sunday morning, after long wrestling in private, I found the Lord with me in my family exercise, wherein my soul's discourse ran upon:

1. The curiosity of man to foreknow what is to come concerning his estate, life, honour, children, and yet man's negligence to use the means of foreknowing the estate of his soul hereafter, and to make our election sure.[2]
2. Our desire to foreknow what would befall this state, church, ourselves, this cause in hand, whether right or wrong, religion or idolatry, peace or war. That the surest, notablest prognostication of what will befall us is the disposition of our own hearts towards our God in all our ways,

---

1 *Diary, 1632–1639*, 313–314.

2 Compare 2 Peter 1:10.

especially in the exercises of his worship and in our private retirings. When they are right within all goes right without; when they are wrong, all goes wrong.[3] As we in them are absent or present with God, we find the Lord absent or present with us in the works of his providence. When our hearts are in a right tune, God lets us see his goodness in his providence; but when it is out of tune, sure that day some evil tidings or other.

And therefore, seeing I found not my heart right that morning, I prognosticated to myself little good; and from the security of the land [and] this city I conjectured some judgement was posting home from the court, as that same night thereafter I heard....

When I was alone at night, I was dejected but got no great access to God...neither then nor on Monday morning, when I read Psalm 112:7–8: "The good man is not, nor shall not, be afraid of evil tidings, his heart is fixed trusting in the Lord, his heart is established, he shall not be afraid, until he see his desire upon his enemies." This reminded [me] of Psalm 59 and 60 wherein some passages are fit for us and proper against our enemies.[4]

---

3 Johnston is deducing a general tendency, not an absolute principle: exceptions undoubtedly occur—his own reading of Scripture the next day reminded him that godly men may receive ill news.

4 These psalms of David plead with God for deliverance, praise his power and pray for judgement upon his enemies.

34

National Covenant renewal[1]

February 23 & 27 and April 1, 1638

Before dinner the insupportable burden of drawing up the Band, whereby all should be linked together after subscribing [to] the Confession of Faith, was laid upon my weak shoulders. So that afternoon...I prayed on my knees earnestly [asking] the Lord to assist, direct, infuse and guide immediately by his Spirit, my heart, hand, tongue and pen in the framing and forming thereof in that manner which might tend most to his glory, this church's welfare, the standing of our religion, laws, liberties and commonwealth, our stricter union with him and amongst ourselves, the greater opposition to idolatry and all other innovations, the instruction of posterity and my own salvation through Christ Jesus....

We got it approved first by the Commissioners [of the Presbytery], then by the whole ministry except one...for which my heart did leap within for joy of this glorious day wherewith our souls would be ravished if they were spiritually disposed. Blessed be the

---

1 *Diary, 1632–1639*, 319, 321–322, 330–332.

name of the eternal God that made my eyes to see the Covenant of the Lord renewed in this land, and far more to have made me, the wickedest…unablest servant to be an instrument in his hand of so great, so gracious, so glorious a work as is this renovation of that national oath of the whole land with our eternal Lord the God of glory. I thanked God from the bottom of my heart for it at home, and feared, a little, some rub from the gentlemen, some stop from the statesmen and bishops, which, O Lord, for thy own name's sake, prevent…that this glorious work of union with thee and communion amongst ourselves may go on and be perfected, which will be the gloriousest day that ever Scotland saw since the Reformation,[2] albeit we should perish for the doing of it.…

Being advertised…of…threats to have my life…I was never dashed at the matter, but went on to write the Bond in parchment, casting my life this way or that way in the hands of my God, the preserver and faithful Redeemer both of my soul and body through Christ Jesus, the God of my salvation.

I heard Mr. Henry Rollock preach on Exodus 19:5 and 8…After [the] sermon…he read all the Covenant over; thereafter he made a pithy exhortation anent[3] the present solemn action of swearing to God. He showed God's part in it out of Jeremiah 3:1…that the Lord was recalling and reclaiming his people, especially this city of Edinburgh, from their former whoredoms and idolatries… and he showed our part out of Luke 15 in the prodigal's returning.…Then he said a very pithy, powerful, pathetic prayer for the Lord's immediate presence, assistance and influence upon this congregation in this most solemn act of worship.…Thereafter he desired the nobles and all the people, stand up unto the Lord, and first desired the noblemen…to hold up their hands and swear…and desired all the people to hold up theirs.…At the instant of rising up and then of holding

---

2 When Scotland, led by John Knox (1510–1572), formally broke with the papacy in 1560.

3 An archaic Scottish word meaning "about" or "concerning."

up their hands, there rose such a yell, such abundance of tears, such a heavenly harmony of sighs and sobs, universally through all the corners of the church, as the like was never seen or heard of. The Spirit of the Lord so filled the sanctuary, warmed the affections, melted the hearts and dissolved the eyes of all the people, men and women, poor and noble, as for a long time they stood still up with their hands up unto the Lord, till Mr. Henry, after he recovered himself, scarce able to speak…closed up all in a heavenly prayer and praise and caused sing Psalm 74:18.

I was moved unto many tears in his first exhortation and prayer before sermon; and in all the time of the solemnity…my heart was like to burst; I got abundance of tears and sobs. Bless the Lord for thy particular motion, but, above all expression, bless his name for that glorious work of his immediate presence and inexpressible influence of the Spirit upon the whole congregation, testifying from heaven that he directed the work, did now bless it and would crown it with some great mercies to which he is, by this lively, powerful, spiritual manner of renewing his covenant, preparing this poor nation, albeit our persons should suffer….The Lord make us never forget his presence in it, but rather make us tell it to our posterity and make us walk worthy of it and within the compass of this Covenant, as Mr. Henry concluded in his prayer, "Give to us, O Lord, what thou askest…then ask what thou wilt." O Edinburgh, Edinburgh, never forget this first day of April, the gloriousest day that ever thou enjoyed. Blessed, ten thousand times blessed, be the name of the eternal God.

35

Responding to national mercies [1]

April 1638

I wrote a letter…of spiritual observations to my Lady Loudon [2] anent [3] the particular motives inducing us to use the present opportunity of God's reconciling the land to himself, pardoning of their backslidings, and renewing his covenant with the land to get our personal and particular pardon, reconciliation and renovation. For, seeing this time in Christian appearance is a new marriage day, at the least is the honeymoon betwixt the Lord and his runaway spouse…let us all, as so many bridesmaids, attend her in these solemn days of swearing and sealing this new contract of marriage, [4] and who knows but the bridegroom will give us some lovetokens of those bracelets [5]…which he in so visible a manner and large a measure is bestowing upon his reconciled spouse in this backsliding

---

1 *Diary, 1632–1639*, 336–337, 340–345.
2 Margaret Campbell, the wife of John, Earl of Loudoun.
3 An archaic Scottish word meaning "about" or "concerning."
4 i.e. the Covenant.
5 Compare Ezekiel 16:11.

kingdom. Seeing this is the time of the Lord's passing by and forgiving our Judah's despising the oath of her covenant[6]...it is a notable opportunity to importune our offended Lord that our personal breaks and backslidings may be wrapped up in that discharge of God to this land, and that general grant of mercy and grace may be particularly assigned...to our soul's...comfort.... Let us therefore both learn and use this happy day of our visitation[7]... let us take even now Rabshakeh's[8] roll of our bygone transgressions...with another catalogue of all our desires, wants, necessities... and present them on our knees to our Lord[9] in this day of his marriage, coronation, reconciliation with the church of Scotland, whereof we are friends, children and members. We never had, nor are likely ever to have, so notable an opportunity of importuning him...for personal mercies or graces, as so many drops of that heavenly shower (now raining down upon whole congregations) upon our withered hearts[10]....

God's wonderful dealing with us either personally or as now nationally, and our... acknowledging it never or seldom go together. Till the well goes dry, we know not whereof the water tastes. The Lord has wrought wonders, yea greater wonders in this land by weaker instruments and in an unliklier way than he wrought either in Egypt by Moses, or Jesus himself did in Judah upon the bodies of men. For in a spiritual sense, may not our Lord's answer to John the Baptist,[11] asking if the Messiah was come, be applied to our Lord's returning to this church, whereby he has made the spiritually blind to see him in the wonders of his law and works of his providence, the spiritually deaf to hear him, like the Lion of the tribe of Judah[12]

---

6 Compare Ezekiel 17:13.
7 Compare Luke 19:44.
8 2 Kings 18
9 Johnston recommends the example of Hezekiah in Isaiah 37:14.
10 Compare Ezekiel 34:25–26.
11 Matthew 11:3–6.
12 Revelation 5:5.

roaring in the threatenings of the law, and like the Lamb of God[13] baying in the calm voice of the gospel; the spiritually dumb... to speak the Shibboleth of our Israel instead of the idiom of Babel,[14] and the spiritually lame to walk... and yet who sets his mind a work or his heart in edge either to consider or admire these spiritual wonders? ...Psalm 107 in all the five instances thereof is a perfect pattern of our case, as the conclusion is of our duty[15]... Lord, make the righteous, his own experimented servants, see it and rejoice, and all iniquity stop her mouth. O that men would praise the Lord for this his...goodness, and for these his bygone wonderful works to this silly, sinful church and nation.[16] ...Shall the Lord take such pains to work a work of wonder for our welfare, and we will not so much as to wear our thoughts upon it or give him thanks for it? I think truly, it straitens[17] the Lord...from raining down the superaffluence of his blessings, and from hastening to crown his work with the capstone, while he looks down and sees not his congregations resounding with the joyful echoes of...heart-ravished thanksgivings, and sees not the families of his saints and their own private personal retirings full of observances and remarks of every circumstance of the footsteps of the Lord....Woe, woe, if by the inobservance of God's ways, as we rob of him of much glory and prevent many future blessings..., so we spoil ourselves of the present use and comfort of God's work....

As for the present estate of our business and our duty...I think truly we are as yet in the mist...I assure myself this church is in her journey out of her Egyptian captivity under human inventions, traditions and injunctions in the worship of God....As yet he has not taken away the pillar of the cloud by day nor the pillar of fire by night,[18] but in all the steps of this her voyage hitherto, he has led

---

13 John 1:29.
14 Judges 12:5–6.
15 Psalm 107:42.
16 Psalm 107: 8,15,21,31.
17 Meaning "restrains."
18 Exodus 13:22.

his reconciled spouse by the hand of his exemplary providence...
As the Lord liveth and reigneth and changeth not...he will not
destroy his inheritance which he has redeemed...he will hear the
prayer of his own Moses, Abrahams and Jacobs in this church, lest
the Egyptians...should say...he was not able to bring them unto
the land which he promised them.[19]...I believe certainly [that] God
in his own time and in his own way and by his own means will
bring to the fruition...that perfect purity of worship and liberty of
discipline in this church.... I am confirmed in this judgement by
the notable speeches of our martyrs and reformers, as Hamilton,
Wishart, Knox.[20]

Read Psalm 78 and 106, Nehemiah 9, and such like. You will
find a very near parallel between Israel and this church, the only
two sworn nations to the Lord.... If you ask what in the time of
our voyage should be our carriage, I will answer in the words of
the apostle, 1 Corinthians 10:5–12...flee from idolatry...as all
human ceremonies...neither let us tempt Christ (by our distrusting
either of his power which is all sufficient or of his goodwill whereof
the shedding of his blood for us being his enemies,[21] his former
inward indulgence and outward providence to this church...are
more than a sufficient proof and pledge). ...Let us even then read
over the history of God's dealing with the Jews.... Let us remark
and eschew whatever in their carriage we find offended the Lord...
and strive to perform all those duties which God then required and
accepted of them by their covenant, and requires from us now in
regard of our covenant with him.

---

19 Compare Deuteronomy 9:26–28.

20 Patrick Hamilton (1504–1528) and George Wishart (1513–1546) were mar-
tyred in St. Andrews, Scotland, for affirming Protestant teachings; John Knox was
Scotland's leading reformer.

21 Romans 5:10.

36

Supplication and consecration [1]

July - August 1638

I meditated on God's former inexpressible goodness to me and my uncomprehensible wickedness against him; on his honouring me, so unworthy a worm, with his own employment...which made me pray that, if it were the Lord's will and that he had no more ado with me, to transport me before I dishonoured him and scandalized my profession and blundered God's former work by my passionate and crooked ways....As I thanked him for procuring himself, and under himself so many clients to me this eight month bygone, so also I begged humbly the Lord's direction whether I should embrace any person's particular employment, lest it distract me from the thoughts of the public business which I should and do prefer to all men's particulars or my own commodity therein.... That, as I have reason to thank God because never man won so much, either benefit or credit or clients in a hundred sessions as I have won this last vacation, so I may have occasion to praise him

---

1   *Diary, 1632–1639*, 354–355, 363–366, 372–373.

for his employing and assisting me in all the particular passages of my calling, especially now…when even I have found my estate and house perishing while the Lord bends my mind and heart solely upon the building of his house….

I got my very heart poured out like water before God in confessing the sins of the church, state, our congregation, family and my own; in recommending the church, state, congregation, family and myself to the Lord; in blessing the Lord for his favours…. Then, when I was praising the Lord for his unspeakable favour in his undeniable providence and assistance to me in his own cause, my heart was mightily stirred up to cry…and conjure the Lord: That, seeing he had elected me to be a vessel of honour before all time; had in my very young years called me to his service…and had continually…reclaimed me from all my wanderings…, I might see this continuance flowed from his mercy…and might tend sensibly to his glory, the welfare of his saints, and my own comfort and increase of grace, that in life and death I might glorify my Lord and be a profitable instrument in Church and Commonwealth, and not an idle drone bee in them and a heavy burden to my friends…. [As the Lord] had settled me in my calling to this end after many scruples, had begun to employ and assist me therein visibly, had now of late above all not only preserved me from manifold temptations and… from outward, gross…offences…but also had deigned… to choose…and assist me as a main instrument in this great work of God in this land…. Seeing the Lord had thus extraordinarily… begun…to glorify himself in my life…[I prayed] that the Lord would not suffer so odd[2] a beginning to have a vile or ordinary end, so fair a preface to have but a common book to back it, so honourable a youth…to end in a dishonourable, unprofitable age. But on the contrary that he…looking back to his own free, free, grace and mercy…would be graciously pleased to continue this odd manner

---

2 Used here to mean "extraordinary" or "remarkable."

of dealing with his unworthy servant, to preserve him in all the rest of his life from public…offences (seeing now thy glory is more interested in my fall) and to glorify his own name in life and death… Thus…sinful dust and ashes durst boldly…cry…with unspeakable confidence and fervency to God as my Father, to my Lord Jesus as my Saviour, to my Sanctifier the Holy Spirit as my director and comforter, with an offer rather to quit all these outward promises and hopes of worldly things…before that by public employments I be drawn on to temptations (wherein my nature will be most slippery… except at every step the Lord immediately hold me by the hand). These hopes and expectations my soul fully…cast over in God's hand, blessing myself that my fortune was not…of my own cutting or carving but in the hand of my gracious, provident God, whose wisdom is infallible, love is unchangeable and power irresistible; that threefold cord on which I hang, as on the surest safest peg, both the salvation of my soul and carriage of my affairs….

I got good…at the hearing of God's sudden hand on my daughter and his safe hand in delivering her again unexpectedly from fainting, and in recommending my family to God…I went in to the old high gallery, and there for a long hour I got extreme great liberty of pouring out my very heart in God's bosom with a sweet shower of melting tears…and with a long, powerful intercourse betwixt the Spirit of God and my soul, ever questioning of the Lord what he demanded and required of me. At every point which the Spirit condescended on…my soul ever echoed back unto him with an earnest petition…as when he instanced that I should seek his face,[3] settle my heart and fix my delight on the light of his countenance,[4] consecrate soul and body to his service, glorify him in my life and death, walk in him…fear the checks of his Spirit, submit my will, family, child, state, name, calling absolutely to his cutting and

---

3 Psalm 27:8.
4 Compare Psalm 37:4; 57:7; 4:6.

carving…to grow in union and communion with him[5].…

My soul rebounded with great fervency a particular petition to each particular demand, as…"O Lord, I desire to seek thy face, make me seek it and find it; I desire to consecrate and employ my soul in thy service, but I cannot; O Lord, thou who only can do it, do it for Christ Jesus sake." After this half hour's continual intercourse…my soul got itself fully disburdened on my God, and was commanded to receive [on] the morrow the sacrament as an infallible pledge of God's glorifying me eternally with himself, and an undoubted gauge of the Lord's glorifying himself in my life and death…and this…particular employment in his own cause which he in his own time will assuredly perfect…yea, as a sure token that the Lord would continue his former manner of dealing with me… perform all his precious promises…and force me…to acknowledge he had done all this and much more.

---

5 Compare Galatians 5:16,25; Colossians 2:6.

37

Asserting Christ's prerogative: speech to the Westminster Assembly[1]

1646

I am a stranger...but as a Christian, under one common Lord, a ruling elder in another church, and a Parliament-man in another kingdom, having commission from both that Church and State, and at the desire of this kingdom...I entreat for your favour and patience to express my thoughts of what is before you.

In my judgement, that is before you[2] which concerns Christ and these kingdoms most and above all, and which will be the chiefest means to end or continue these troubles[3]...I can neither be persuaded that they were raised for, or will be calmed upon the

---

1 The full text of this speech is in John Howie, *The Scots Worthies* (1775; Repr. Edinburgh: The Banner of Truth Trust, 1995), 303–308.

2 The Westminster Assembly was considering the Long Parliament's proposals to appoint civil commissioners to hear appeals in cases of church discipline.

3 Johnston is referring to the civil wars and unsettlement.

settlement of civil rights and privileges, either of kings or princes, whatsoever may seem to be our present success; but I am convinced they have a higher rise from, and for the highest end, the settling of the Crown of Christ in these islands, to be propagated from island to continent; and until King Jesus be set down on his throne, with his sceptre in his hand, I do not expect God's peace.... But establish that and a durable peace will be found to follow.... Let us lay to heart what is before us.... Let us both tremble and rejoice[4] when we reflect upon what is under debate, and now in our hands.

...All Christians are bound to give a testimony to every truth when called to it, but ye are the immediate servants of the Most High, Christ's proctors and heralds, whose proper function it is to proclaim his name, preserve his offices and assert his rights. Christ has had many testimonies given to his prophetical and priestly offices by the pleadings and sufferings of his saints, and in these latter days seems to require the same unto his kingly office.... Although Christ's kingdom be not of this world...yet it is in this world, and for this end was he born.[5] To give a testimony to this truth, among others, were we born, and must not be ashamed of it, nor deny it; but confess and avouch it,[6] by pleading, doing and suffering for it, even when what is in agitation seems most to oppose it...let all know that the Spirit of your Master is upon you, and that Christ hath servants who will not only make pulpits to ring with the sound of his prerogative, but also, if they shall be called to it, to make a flame of their bodies burning at the stake for a testimony to it, ...that *Christ lives and reigns alone in his Church*, and will have all done therein according to his word and will, and that he has given no supreme headship over his Church to any Pope, King or Parliament whatsoever.

---

4 Compare Psalm 2:11.

5 John 18:36–37.

6 Compare the commands and warnings of 2 Timothy 1:8; 2:12; Mark 8:38; Matthew 10:32–33.

...The covenant begins with the advancement, and ends with the enlargement of the kingdom of Christ....And all laws contrary to the will of Christ are acknowledged to be void in his kingdom.... Christ's throne is highest, and his privileges supreme as only King and Head of his Church, albeit kings and magistrates may be members in it. There is no authority to be balanced with his.... Is it so small a thing to have the sword, but they must have the keys also?[7]... I am confident that the Parliament, and both nations, will acknowledge themselves engaged under this authority....

...I am confident that whatever diversity of opinion may be among you in any particular, you will all hold out Christ's kingdom distinct from the kingdoms of the earth, and that he has appointed the government of his own house, and should rule the same; and that none of this Assembly, even for the gaining of their desires in all the points of difference, would, by their silence, concealment and connivance, weaken, commutate, or sell a part of this fundamental truth, this sovereign interest of Christ; and that you will all concur to demonstrate the same, by clear passages of Scripture, or necessary consequences therefrom, and by constant practice of the apostles, which are rules unto us....

---

7   The keys of the kingdom of heaven, entrusted by Christ to his church. See Matthew 16:19.

38

Counsel to Charles II [1]

1650-1651

Remember the grounds of my letter—that he make Christ's cause upmost and not his crown, and use lawful means and instruments, join covenant and reconcilement with God, a covenanted and converted king.... That he seek fellowship with God...follow the advice of God's servants...suspect all counsels...that would separate him...and the Church of God...I cannot serve God and him with a good conscience without private freedom to him, which his father took not ill but well, as he told [me] when he made me King's Advocate at Newcastle. [2]

...Let there be Christian order kept in his family, and as well that himself keep public ordinance, family service and private devotion... Let all about or under him follow his example in satisfying the Church, discountenance all profanity and profane persons at his court, and let religion have credit in it and God's servants be

---

1   D.H. Fleming, ed., *The Diary of Sir Archibald Johnston of Wariston, 1650–1654* (Edinburgh: Scottish History Society, 1919), 23–24, 131–132.

2   Charles I bestowed this senior judicial post on Johnston in October 1646.

encouraged....The King took well what I said, and desired me to use freedom with himself. I pressed much his private reading the Word and private prayer....

I begged the Lord might humble our King and those with him before the Lord himself, and that before the decree come forth and the black day of reckoning with them overtake them.... As we came out of kirk, we heard all the cannons of the castle and ships shoot, and learned that it was for the total rout of the Scots army[3]...which made me cry to the Lord. O how true is the Lord in his threatenings and terrible in his judgements.... How often has this ruin been foretold by his servants, that durst not run on in the same course of defection! How did the Lord assist me at Perth, in the reasons of my protestation to forewarn the King, being present, and the Committee,[4] that the Lord, seeing this discovery of our sins written in the blood of the commons contemned, would write it in the highest and best blood there, that it might be more legible, and pressed upon the King...what Joab said to David (2 Samuel 19:6–7), that because he loved his enemies and hated his friends, a worse thing would befall him then ever till then, and begged the Lord might give him a sight of his personal sins and of his father's house, and that by repentance he might break off the Lord's controversy against them.... This strange passage remembers me of that of the prophet anent[5] Coniah[6] ...and of my letter to him in Holland,[7] showing that his dissembled incoming to the Covenant would sooner ruin him than his father's twelve years opposition[8] ruined him. But strange has been and is the idolatry of this land and people.

---

3 By Oliver Cromwell (1599–1658) at the Battle of Worcester, September 3, 1651.

4 The Committee of Estates, the executive appointed by the Scottish Parliament.

5 An archaic Scottish word meaning "about" or "concerning."

6 Jeremiah 22:24–30.

7 Where Charles had negotiated the treaty of Heligoland with the Covenanters, under which he reluctantly, and with patent insincerity, took the Covenants.

8 1637–1649.

39

Personal and familial covenanting[1]

1651-1654

This Wednesday, June 18 [1651] the Lord pressed on my mind...to renew my covenant for me and my seed with him again...whereupon...I did dedicate, consecrate, resign and give over soul and body, all the faculties of the one and members of the other, either of myself, wife, or bairns[2] and their seed in their generations, to the Father, the Son, the Spirit.... As I would have gladly had the covenants made between my predecessors and the Lord for us, their seed, especially those made by my two grandmothers and my mother with the Lord, to the fore, that always in my straits and trials I might have presented the same to the Lord...so I conjure my seed to spread this seventh covenant of mine, as also the former six with the Lord, before him, for mercy and grace and blessing from him....

On Sunday morning, April 4 [1652], intending to baptize my

---

1 *Diary, 1650–1654*, 68, 152-153, 280.
2 A Scottish expression for "children."

daughter Janet, I did read in my family, Genesis 17:6-15, then Psalm 89:25–38…and I prayed heartily thereupon for my family and for the young infant, that we might find the good of the covenant and these promises made good to us.… Between sermons, in private, I offered up my little daughter to the Lord, as heartily and freely, and presented and consecrated her to be the Lord's in soul and body, life and death, as I had presented any of the rest before to him.… In church…my soul…remembered[3] the Lord of my particular covenant before, seven times renewed with him, for me and my seed. Upon which the Lord brought to my mind and put it in my heart to make this the eighth solemn time of renewing it at this sacrament…and that for myself, my wife, and my nine children, whom there I named to the Lord, Archibald, John, Sanders,[4] Elizabeth, Rachel, Helen, Margret, Anna and now Janet, all whom in the church I inwardly from my soul devoted…unto the Lord.…

[July 6, 1654] At night I got Mr. William Guthrie's tract[5] anent[6] personal formal soul covenanting, and adored and blessed God when I read it that ever God put that business in my heart, and made me communicate and press it on others, as a greater favour than if the Lord had given to me the ownership of the whole earth. I pray the Lord to bless that tract and exercise to many of his in these sad times.

---

3 Meaning "reminded."

4 Alexander.

5 William Guthrie, *The Christian's Great Interest.* William Guthrie (1620–1665) was minister of the church at Fenwick, Scotland.

6 An archaic Scottish word meaning "about" or "concerning."

40

Enduring hardship [1]

April - May 1654

I fear my wife's sickliness, who is always telling me that I will not think her in danger till she be gone. The Lord my God preserve her and pity my condition in her case, who can neither care for myself nor my bairns[2] nor affairs, and has no body in the world that would care for me and them.[3] The Lord spare, sanctify my wife, make her good and make her well.... The Lord preserve my children and family from sins and scandals, and the Lord provide for them.... I met with my wife's discontent upon folks' speeches at my lowness, because of a tailor boy following me...I got liberty from the Lord to pray...that if he would have me more vile yet for his name and by new oppressions of me for my testimony...let me be yet more evil, though it were not only to go without a manservant but also to become a man or servant to others[4]....

---

1 *Diary, 1650–1654*, 228–229, 235–236, 245, 247, 249.
2 A Scottish expression for "children."
3 Compare Psalm 142:4.
4 Compare David's response to his wife Michal's criticism in 2 Samuel 6:22.

At the grace after dinner, I found my wife mightily moved to tears and groans, which made me insist the more on suits for mercy and grace, and she went to her bed and I found her oppressed with grief.... She apprehended I and my family were ruined in our estate,[5] and she wished to be out of the world as one cause of it as she said. I pressed her to be earnest with the Lord for mercy to her, and to me and to our children.... Getting assurance of his reconcilement, let us beg his grace to be honest, faithful, upright and constant to him in private fellowship and public serviceableness, and let us submit to him anent[6] our outward condition, and be content with whatsoever lot he send, how strait, mean, low, sore soever it may seem to our flesh and blood. And if we do so, the Lord would either deliver us from our straits and distresses, or sanctify them to us[7]....

I prayed in the morning on 2 Thessalonians 3:7–12 about the apostle's diligence in his calling and working that he might eat. The Lord tell me in what calling he appoints me to work and to eat, for all my callings almost are taken from me but one—of testifying and suffering. "Lord, enable me to be faithful in these, and provide for me and mine what is necessary and convenient. I see, by thy works of justice, thou art a living, reigning God."...In grace and prayer I begged for a sight of a vain world, our wicked self, and our good God through the Mediator; and I begged that the Lord would count all mine his, and that I might count all his mine. Alas! habitually we neglect God and ourselves, when all things go according to our mind, and so force the Lord to remove them from us or let us perish.... The Lady Inglestoun said she had faith that none of my children would beg; and I said I desired submission even to their begging, if he would be with them in it and make it the means of his greater glory and their greater fellowship and

---

5 Johnston's conscientious opposition to the English conquest had resulted in unemployment and the loss of much money and status.

6 An archaic Scottish word meaning "about" or "concerning."

7 Compare James 4:7; Hebrews 13:5; 1 Timothy 6:8.

serviceableness....When I went to bed my thoughts ran on Psalm 37:4, "Delight thyself in the Lord and thou shalt have the desires of thine heart," of that renewed heart that delights in the Lord, for these must be on things tending to God's glory and our fellowship with him, and means and ways of increasing our delight in God, even as a heart that delights in profits or honours or pleasures has its desires on things, means and ways tending thereunto. And if God grant me the desires of a renewed heart delighting in God, what though he deny me all the desires of the unrenewed heart that were hindrances thereunto...

Walking in the [Scheins] Yard I considered it was above twenty years since I had walked in many an exercise in that alley, and had found many changes since 1633, and received many proofs of the Lord's attributes and promises and words in his works...and that he had put many employments on me, countenanced them with influences and backed them with blessings, and now had taken away his public, state employments, yet by his influences and providences let me see...that I had as good and great reason to bless God when he took them away as when he gave them.[8]

---

8 Compare Job 1:21.

41

Attempting godly correction [1]

June - August 1654

Mr. John Oliphant[2] told me of the high, proud, unruly spirit of Archibald[3]...Mr. Robert Douglas[4] told me of his miscarriage to him with an oath, and heard of another when he was out at Wariston, and of his haunting the company of Dalmahoy's sons who are great swearers. I thought I heard the description of my own youthly humour, passion and fury, my own picture and nature in his temper. "O Lord, restrain it and renew it for thy name's sake, and direct my spirit in thy fear to worship thee, and to educate him who having often been dedicated to thee, and now deserted of thee is raged in the more by Satan. O Lord, sanctify him; O Lord, pass over his youth without a mark or complaint. O Lord, tell me thy mind anent[5] my duty to thee concerning my child...." We read

---

1 *Diary, 1650–1654,* 271–272, 278, 297.
2 The tutor assigned to Archibald, Jr.
3 Archibald was Johnston's eldest surviving son and heir, then aged fifteen.
4 The local minister.
5 An archaic Scottish word meaning "about" or "concerning."

after dinner Mark 2…and then I spoke to my son in private, discharged him from going unto the company of Dalmahoy's sons… remembered[6] him of his covenant to God, pressed on him duty to God and man. The Lord God put it and keep it in his heart continually. I told him I had nothing to give him with the rest; what I had I would give to those that had most of the fear of God. I prayed when he was gone that the Lord would make something keep impression in him…. I told him that as the Lord made me devote him to God, and get it under his own hand, and to pray often for him, so I thought either the Lord would make use of him and bless him or would plague him eminently…. My heart was sore to sin lying on us all, master, mistress, child, servant; and the Lord's hand on our calling, name, estate, as ruined and going to utter ruin…

I heard of Archibald's biding from the school and being in the company of Dalmahoy's sons, debauched lads. The Lord direct me without passion to take the right course how to reclaim or correct him for thy name's sake…. At night I spoke again to my son Archibald, before his mother, and gave him warnings to follow his book and abstain from ill company and everything that is scandalous…

I spoke my mind sharply to my wife and her daughter[7] against their promiscuous dancing at the marriage; and was glad to see it affect my daughter. The Lord bless this ordinance to them and to me too. Lord, forgive and cure the negligent and humorous temper of my son.[8]

---

6 Meaning "reminded."

7 Elizabeth, Johnston's eldest child.

8 Sadly, this prayer was not granted: Archibald Jr.'s condition deteriorated into insanity, which was a great grief to Johnston and his wife.

42

Looking back and forward [1]

January 5, 1656

I thought that from the fifteenth year of my age till twenty-two was
my private youth; from twenty-two to twenty-seven...was my
private life; from twenty-seven to forty...was my thirteen years of
public life; from that till forty-six now near, my private retired life
for five years even as it was other five years private before my public
employment. I thought if God would give me another thirteen
years of a public [life], even by course of nature, I would be near
my end.... I desire and do offer before heaven and earth and his
angels my service once again for his public interests and friends
unto the Lord my God in Christ Jesus, and if he thinks not fit to
employ me my request is with Barzillai for my sons and daughters
to be employed by him;[2] and, in the meantime, that he would send
by what hand he will bless to his poor people, and I shall desire to
pray for a blessing to them and to his instruments for them. Only

1   J.D. Ogilvie, ed., *The Diary of Sir Archibald Johnston of Wariston, 1655–1660*
(Edinburgh: Scottish History Society, 1940), 21–22.

2   2 Samuel 19:37; 1 Kings 2:7.

I desire now to table this my offer on the condition and terms of his own grace.... Many have thought I have been born for a blessing or a curse, and the most part thinks I am born for a plague to thy church and interests. Leave me not to verify the sayings of enemies as so many prophecies. If I live not to do good, my nature is such as it will be doing much evil.

43

Considering renewed service[1]

1656-1657

I never was about so ticklish a business and dangerous[2] and of greater consequence in the right or wrong doing of it to God, his friends and interests.... "Lord let me not go if I go not resolved against sinful compliances, and if I go not resolved for restraint and suffering for testimony to thy name."...I resolve by God's grace not to disclaim but to adhere to my former testimony against the war, the conquest, the government as founded thereon and a toleration in ecclesiastical matters. I resolve not to meddle with engagements to stand or fall with them and to maintain their power[3]...and not to be farther for them than they shall turn out to be for God and in the conditional subordinate terms of the Covenant.... I resolve to meddle in no state employments except it were a commission

---

1 *Diary, 1655–1660*, 41–43, 71, 77–88.

2 In September 1656, Johnston was considering a visit to London and had contacted the Lord Protector, Oliver Cromwell, who was eager to overcome his opposition to the regime; arrest was a distinct possibility if he remained obdurate.

3 The English government required such oaths of officeholders.

as to Ezra, Nehemiah, Zerubbabel, to build the house of God and settle and further Christ's interests; or a commission to honest men to see all the magistrates were appointed of godly men in the terms agreed to, and to rule the people according to their own laws of church and state, only they paying tribute and keeping garrisons, till the Lord should change the heart of our conquerors to let us be free, living in friendship with our neighbours....

"Dear Lord, if anything in this be a going further than thou allowest, discover it to me and scrape it out and let it never be heard of nor suffer us to be tempted in it.". . . There inclines me to go, the great straits of his work, and people weakening, fainting, and failing daily, and my earnest desire, if the Lord would honour me again, to be in public service instrumental for the good of his affairs and people...I cannot deny my desire to use the means of getting my own for maintenance of my family...and then some secret hints and hopes of God's reviving his work and people in this seventh year of their captivity, which used to be the year of release[4]... But however it go with me, the Lord revive his work and people. That which fears and shakes me most...is the fear of a conjuncture of my corruption and outward temptations of baits and straits...and the Lord's desertion of me to sinful compliances contrary to the Word, my covenants, principles, testimonies...expectations of the godly, vows to God and letters to men, providential temple words recorded in my diary, many expressions in family prayer and in exercises at conference and prayer....

After the Protector's government [was] settled by [an] Act of Parliament and consent of nations as much as any conqueror was,[5] I think it as lawful to take places from him as King James. "Render

---

4 An allusion to the Year of Jubilee. See Deuteronomy 31:10; Exodus 21:2.

5 In 1657 Cromwell was reinstalled as Lord Protector under a new constitution devised by a parliament that included representatives of Scotland and Ireland, as well as England.

to Caesar the things that are Caesar's'"[6]…give to thy king or emperor (whom ye question for usurpation) the things that belong to a king, as unto God the things due to any God… I see not men's being useful in their generation[7] by laying aside upon discontent as by endeavouring in any capacity what they can…. Is not Cromwell without the Malignants[8] better than Charles with them, which is the real state of the question?…

He [Cromwell] made a long discourse of his intentions and good affections towards the Remonstrators,[9] and his desire of a union between that godly party there and…these here, and said it was not well done in differences to look only to one part or party. He asked if I was clear and free to serve and take employments, and I said I was free in things lawful and conducible to the service of God and his people and his highness therein.

---

6 Matthew 22:21.
7 Compare Acts 13:36.
8 The Royalist/Episcopalian party, notorious, like Charles II, for ungodliness.
9 Johnston's minority faction in the Kirk.

44

Retirement and disaster [1]

1659-1660

Alas for my confederating and associating with that Army[2] which had been unfaithful…to God and man; and abetting them in their unlawful courses….It would be a strange and wonderful act, if the Lord made these men,[3] yet for all that's past…to call me to their counsels, and I will readily obey it and say I followed God's call, and why not as well when in an ordinary and unanimous way they lay me aside and leave me out, I should say God calls me to retire and I will go cheerfully about it…

Whereas I thought I was following the call of God's providence…. the truth is I followed the call of providence when it agreed with my humour and pleased my idol and seemed to tend to honour and advantage. But if that same providence had called me to quit

---

1 *Diary, 1655–1660*, 165-166, 180, 183.

2 The English army under General John Lambert (1619–1684), which expelled the Long Parliament in October 1659, despite engagements to obey it, was forced to readmit it in December.

3 The restored Members of Parliament.

my better places and take me to meaner places or none at all, I had not so hastily and contentedly followed it, as appeared by my great despondency and melancholy when I thought the Council of State[4] was taking my old idol, Clerk Registership,[5] from me, and my great lightness, vanity, frothyness, upliftedness of mind and raisedness of heart when I was called to the Council and to preside…and then when I was made and kept on to be President of the Committee[6] so as I never seriously pressed the change of it.…And now the Lord punishes my ambition…[causes] General Monck[7] to accuse me as the incendiary of these nations both at home and abroad, and to seek my place to his good brother… And hereupon some heavy, bitter words of my wife's to me for my meddling with this Committee and my passionate reply that I found her often a miserable comforter to me in the day of my calamity;[8] my heart was like to break and burst with grief.…

The face of affairs now presently looks very dark.…He will light my candle (which is now gone out with a snuffle…) and enlighten my darkness[9]…a word which I should never forget, because it was the last word which my mother spake on earth.…The Lord knows that in the Council and Committee of Safety I had some good purposes through his grace towards God's covenant, work and people in Scotland.…Mr. Robert Burnet[10] told me with Christian freedom of men's speaking to have my life, and that because I was

---

4 The powerful executive appointed by the restored Long Parliament in May 1659.

5 An important office to which Johnston had aspired since 1640; he attained it in 1649, lost it in 1651 and then regained it from Cromwell in 1657.

6 The Committee of Safety, the feeble and short-lived executive appointed by the army in October 1659.

7 Commander of the English army in Scotland, George Monck (1608–1670) had successfully opposed Parliament's expulsion, and was now marching on London; he would soon preside over the restoration of Charles II.

8 Job 16:2.

9 Psalm18:28.

10 Johnston's brother-in-law.

the cause of all the blood in Scotland…and that they desire my blood and do not hear of my being in any place again….The Lord knows I deserve it not from my nation, to whom I had a great respect and a great desire to do them good and gain their respect.

45

A final testimony:
his speech from the scaffold [1]

July 22, 1663

Right Honourable, much honoured and beloved Auditors and Spectators—that which I intended and prepared to have spoken at this time…is not at present in my power, being taken from me when apprehended…yet I bless the Lord…I am in any capacity to leave this weak and short Testimony.

1. I desire in the first place to confess my sins…and to acknowledge God's Mercies; and to express my repentance of the one, and my faith of the other, through the merits of the Lord Jesus Christ, our gracious Redeemer and Mediator. I confess that my natural temper hath been hasty and passionate, and that in my manner of going about…the best pieces of work and service to the Lord and to my Generation, I have been subject to my excesses of heat, and thereby

---

1 *The last discourse of the Right Honourable the Lord Warestoune, as he delivered it upon the scaffold at the Mercat-Cross of Edinburgh, July 22, 1663, being immediately before his death* (Edinburgh, 1664), 5–9.

to some precipitations, which have no doubt offended standers-by…
and exposed both me and the work to their mistakes; whereby the
beauty of that Work hath been much obscured. Neither have I in
following the Lord's Work, his Good Work, been altogether free of
self-seeking, to the grief of my own conscience, which hath made
me oftentimes to cry out with the Apostle, "O wretched man that
I am, who shall deliver me from this body of death?"[2] and to lie low
in the dust, mourning and lamenting over the same, deprecating
God's Wrath and begging his tender Mercies to pardon, and his
powerful Grace to cure all these evils.…

2. I dare not deny on the other hand, but must testify in the second
place, to the glory of his free Grace, that the Lord my God hath
often shewed, ensured into and engraven upon my conscience the
Testimony of his reconciled Mercy, through the Merits of Jesus
Christ, pardoning all my iniquities, and assuring me that he would
deliver me also by the Grace of his Holy Spirit, from the spite,
tyranny and dominion thereof, and hath often drawn forth my
spirit to the exercise of Repentance and Faith, and hath often
engraven upon my heart in legible characters, the merciful pardoning and gracious-begun cure thereof, to be perfected thereafter to
the glory of his Name, Salvation of my own soul, and Edification
of his Church.

3. I am pressed in conscience to leave here at my death, my true
and honest Testimony in the sight of God and man, unto and for the
National Covenant, the Solemn League and Covenant, the solemn
Acknowlegements of our Sins and Engagements to our Duties, and
to all Grounds and Causes of Fasts and Humiliations, and of the
Lord's Displeasure and Contendings with the Land, and to the
several Testimonies given for his Interests by General Assemblies,

---

2 Romans 7:24.

Commissions of the Kirk, Synods, Presbyteries and other faithful Ministers and Professors.

4. I am also pressed to encourage his doing, suffering, witnessing People…that they would continue in their duties of mourning, praying, believing, witnessing and sympathizing with others, and humbly to assure them in the Name of the Lord our God, the God of his own Word and Work, of his Covenant, Cause and People, that he will be seen, found and felt in his own gracious way and time, by his own means and instruments, for his own honour and glory, to return to his own Truths, Interests and Servants, to revive his Name, his Covenant, his Word, his Work, his Sanctuary and his Saints in this Nation, yea even in these three Covenanted Nations, which were by so solemn Bonds [and] Covenants…devoted to himself.

5. I exhort all those that have been, or are, enemies or unfriendly to the Lord's Name, Covenant or Cause, Word, Work or People… to repent and amend before these sad Judgements…come upon them for their sinning so highly against the Lord, because of any temptations of the time…by baits or straits whatsoever, and that after so many Engagements and professions of not a few of themselves to the contrary.

6. I dare not conceal from you who are friendly to all the Lord's precious Interests…that the Lord (to the commendation of his Grace, be it humbly spoken) hath several times in the exercise of my Repentance and Faith (during my troubles) and after groans and tears upon these three notable chapters, *viz.* the ninth of Ezra, ninth of Nehemiah, and the ninth of Daniel, together with other suitable Scriptures, even in the very nick of humble and fervent prayers… for reviving again of his Name, Covenant, Cause, Word and Work of Reformation in these Covenanted Nations, and

particularly in poor Scotland…that the Lord, I say, hath several times given me good grounds of hope and lively expectations of his merciful, gracious, powerful, and wonderful renewing, reviving again of all his former great interests…in such a way…as shall wonderfully rejoice his mourning Friends, and astonish his contradicting and contra-acting Enemies.

7. I do earnestly recommend my poor afflicted Wife and Children, and their Posterity, to the choicest Blessings of God, and unto the Prayers and Favours of all the Lord's Children and Servants…that they may not be ruined for my sake, but that for the Lord my God's sake they may be favoured, assisted, supplied and comforted; and may also be fitted for his Fellowship and Service, whom God himself hath moved so often in their own presence, and with their own consents, to dedicate, devote, resign, alike and as well as I devoted and resigned my own soul unto him for all time and eternity.

8. Now, here I beseech the Lord to open the eyes of all the Instruments of my Trouble, who are not deadly irreconcilable Enemies to himself and his People, that they may see the Wrong done by them to himself and his People…and to Me and Mine, and may repent thereof, return to the Lord, and more cordially maintain, own and adhere unto all his Interests in time to come. The Good Lord give unto them Repentance, Remission and Amendment, which is the worst wish I do, and the best wish I can, wish unto them; for I can wish no better to myself.

9. I do most humbly and earnestly beg the Fervent Prayers of his Praying Children, Servants and Instruments, wheresoever they be… to be put up in behalf of his Name, Cause, Covenant, Work and People…and that the Lord would Glorify himself, Edify his Church, Encourage his Saints further and accomplish his [good work] by all his Doings and Dealings, in substances towards all his own.

10. Whereas I heard that some of my own Friends have…defamed my name,…I am free…from any accession, by counsel or contrivance, or any other way to his late Majesty's death, or to their making that change of the Government; and the Lord judge between Me and mine Accusers: and I pray the Lord to preserve the present King, his Majesty, and to pour his best Blessings upon him….

11. I do here submit and commit my Soul and Body, Wife and Children, and their Children's Children, from Generation to Generation for ever, with all others our Lord's Friends and Followers, and all his doing, suffering, witnessing, sympathizing Ones, in the present and subsequent Generations, unto the Lord's choicest Mercies, Graces, Favours, Services, Employments, Empowerments, Enjoyments, Improvements and Inheritances, in Earth and Heaven, in Time and Eternity. Which suits, with all others which he hath at any time by his Spirit moved and assisted me to make and put up according to his Will, I leave before the Throne, and upon the Father's merciful bowels, and the Son's mediating Mercies, and the Holy Spirit's compassionate groans, for now and for evermore. Amen.

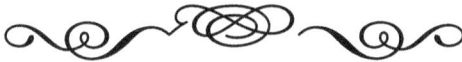

Select bibliography

Donald, P.H. "Archibald Johnston of Wariston and the Politics of Religion." *Records of the Scottish Church History Society.* 1990–1992, 123–140.

Howie, James. *The Scots Worthies.* 1775. Reprint, Edinburgh: The Banner of Truth Trust, 1995.

Johnston, Archibald. *The Diary of Sir Archibald Johnston of Wariston, 1632–1639.* Edited by G.M. Paul. Edinburgh: Scottish History Society, 1911.

Johnston, Archibald. *The Diary of Sir Archibald Johnston of Wariston, 1650–1654.* Edited by D.H. Fleming. Edinburgh: Scottish History Society, 1919.

Johnston, Archibald. *The Diary of Sir Archibald Johnston of Wariston, 1655–1660.* Edited by J.D. Ogilvie. Edinburgh: Scottish History Society, 1940.

Johnston, Archibald. *The last discourse of the Right Honourable the Lord Warestoune, as he delivered it upon the scaffold at the Mercat-Cross of Edinburgh, July 22, 1663, being immediately before his death.* Edinburgh, 1664.

Morrill, John, editor. *The Scottish National Covenant in its British Context, 1638–1651.* Edinburgh: Edinburgh University Press, 1990.

Omond, George W. T. *The Lord Advocates of Scotland From the Close of the Fifteenth Century to the Passing of the Reform Bill.* Edinburgh: David Douglas, 1883.

Stevenson, David. *King or Covenant?: Voices from Civil War.* East Linton: Tuckwell Press, 1996.

Stevenson, David. *Revolution and Counter-Revolution in Scotland, 1644–1651.* Edinburgh: John Donald, 2003.

Stevenson, David. *The Scottish Revolution, 1637–1644: The Triumph of the Covenanters.* Newton Abbott: David & Charles Press, 1973.

Wodrow, Robert. *The History of the Sufferings of the Church of Scotland from the Restoration to the Revolution.* 1721/1722. Reprint, Glasgow: Blackie, Fullarton, & Co., 1829.

Yeoman, Louise. "Archie's invisible worlds discovered: spirituality, madness and Johnston of Wariston's family." *Records of the Scottish Church History Society.* 1997.

Reading spiritual classics

by Michael A.G. Haykin, series editor

In recent days, "spirituality" has become something of a buzzword in Reformed circles. This is all well and good. But there is a downside to the story. The spiritual books being read are often drawn from streams that are seriously deficient when it comes to the truths in which Reformed believers delight. This series has been designed to partially fill the gap by providing choice selections from various Reformed writers.

The reading of spiritual classics should differ from other types of reading. Whereas one reads a newspaper, dictionary or textbook for factual information or immediate answers to queries, in spiritual reading one seeks to inflame the heart as well as to inform the mind. Spiritual reading, as Eugene Peterson has noted, should therefore be "leisurely, repetitive, reflective reading." It should not be hurried, for attention needs to be paid to what the Spirit of God is saying through the text. And texts rich in spiritual nourishment beg to be read again and again so that their truth and beauty might be savoured.

Of course, when it comes to spiritual classics, the Bible occupies a unique and indispensable place. It is the fountainhead and source of the Christian faith. Anyone wishing to make progress as a disciple of Christ must be committed to regular reflection and meditation on the Scriptures. Blessed is the believer whose delight is in the Word of God, on which he or she "meditates day and night" (Psalm 1:1–2).

But we are neither the first to read the Scriptures nor the first to meditate extensively on them. Christians of previous days also found strength and nourishment by meditating on the Word of God. Often their wisdom and insight was recorded—either in books, diaries, letters, hymns or sermons—and these, having been preserved, we are in the habit of calling spiritual classics. Such classics have a way of sending their readers back to the Bible with deeper insight into the nature of the Christian faith and cultivate a greater desire to seek after Christ's glory and blessed presence.

Other titles available from Joshua Press…

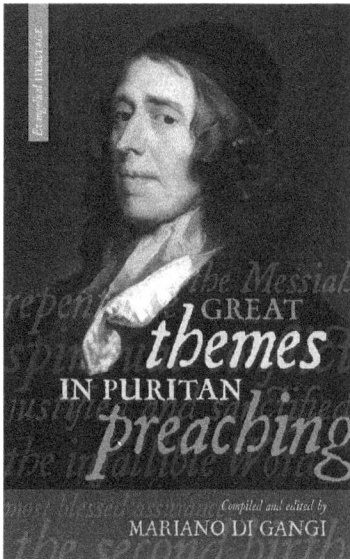

Great themes in Puritan preaching

Compiled and edited
By Mariano Di Gangi

DRAWING FROM a gold mine of Puritan writings, this book provides a taste of the riches of Puritan theology and its application to life. This title will whet your appetite and stir your faith to greater views of Christ, his Person and his work.

ISBN 978–1-894400-26–8 (HC)

ISBN 978-1-894400-24–4 (PB)

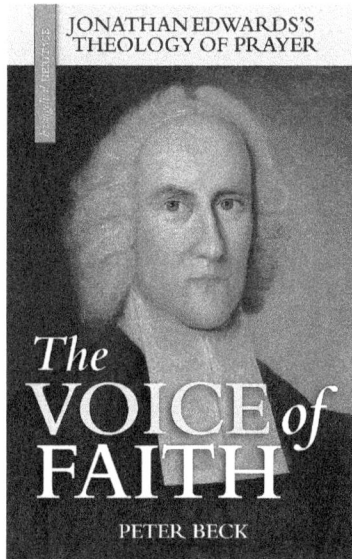

The voice of faith
Jonathan Edwards's theology of prayer
By Peter Beck

EXPLORING THE sermons and writings of Jonathan Edwards, Dr. Beck draws a comprehensive picture of his theology of prayer and why Edwards believed God would hear the prayers of his people. Interspersed are three external biographies that set the historical and theological scene.

ISBN 978–1-894400-33–6 (HC)

ISBN 978-1-894400-32–9 (PB)

Other titles available from Joshua Press...

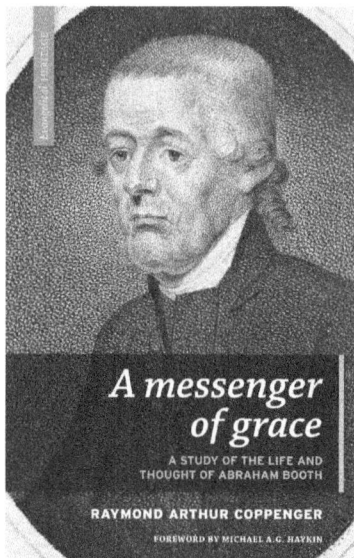

A messenger of grace
A study of the life and thought of Abraham Booth
By Raymond A. Coppenger

ABRAHAM BOOTH, a spiritual giant in eighteenth-century Baptist life, was a leading London pastor and theologian. Deeply respected for his living faith, wise counsel, evangelistic zeal and perceptive writing, his influential life and thought are awakened for a new audience.

ISBN 978–1-894400-31–2

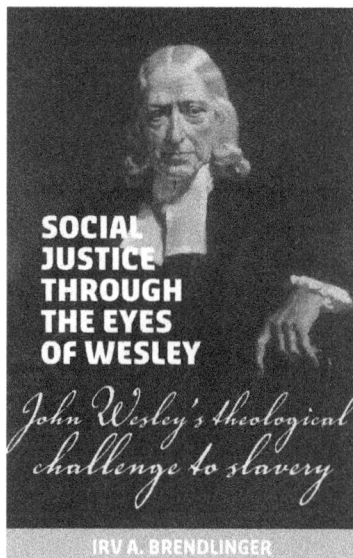

Social justice through the eyes of Wesley
John Wesley's theological challenge to slavery
By Irv Brendlinger

JOHN WESLEY was the first Christian leader of world renown to take a decisive stand against slavery. With wide-ranging analysis and depth, this book shows how Wesley's convictions compelled him to labour tirelessly for abolition.

ISBN 978–1-894400-23–7

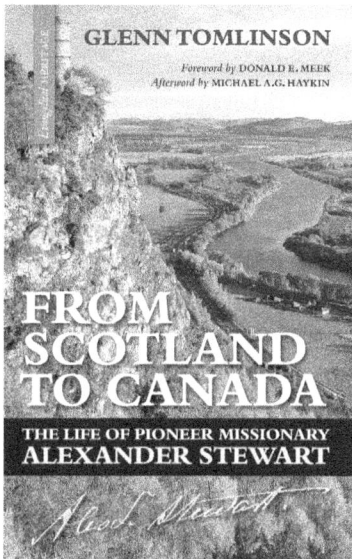

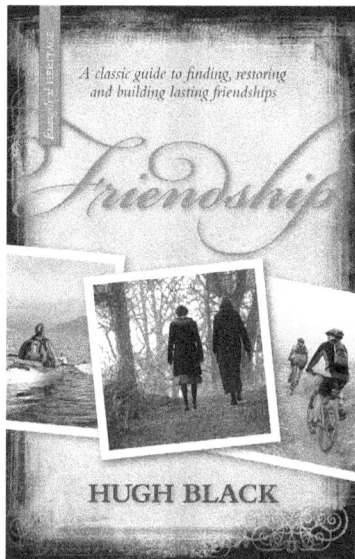

From Scotland to Canada

The life of
pioneer missionary
Alexander Stewart
By Glenn Tomlinson

ALEXANDER STEWART'S story is
one of persistent zeal for the
extension of God's kingdom
and a fervent desire to do what
he could to bring the gospel to
a young country, founding the
first Baptist church in York
(Toronto). His pioneer heart
left a deep mark on Canada.

ISBN 978–1–894400–29–9

Friendship

By Hugh Black

HUGH BLACK addresses the chal-
lenges and responsibilities of
friendship, including the consequences of wrecked friendships.
In true friendship, accountabil-
ity and love inspire us to live
with more honour, integrity
and grace. Ultimately, we see
that in Jesus Christ we can have
that "higher friendship," which
revolutionizes the way we live
and think, and what we value.

ISBN 978-1-894400-28-2 (HC)
ISBN 978-1-894400-27-5 (PB)

Deo Optimo et Maximo Gloria
To God, best and greatest, be glory

joshua
press

www.joshuapress.com